ARE YOU READY?
The Final Wake-Up Call Before Time Runs Out

By T.A. Braddock

For permissions or speaking requests:
lifteverylife@gmail.com

First Edition: 2025 • Printed in the United States of America
ISBN: 979-8-9925035-2-4
Published by: Lift Every Life Solutions, LLC

Acknowledgments

This book was forged in the secret place, but it would not exist without the people God placed in my life along the way.

To my family—thank you for loving me, encouraging me, and giving me the space to chase the call of God with everything I've got.

To my church family—you showed me what it means to burn for Jesus. Your hunger ignited mine.

To every preacher, evangelist, and revivalist who came before me—you lit the torch. I'm just trying to carry it faithfully.

To my editors, friends, and early readers—your insights made this book better, your prayers made it anointed, and your belief made it possible.

And finally, to Jesus Christ—my Redeemer, King, and closest friend. You gave me a message. You gave me fire. You gave me grace I could never earn. May this book make You famous.

Table of Contents

Author's Welcome

Before We Begin: A Personal Word from the Author

You're holding more than just a book. This is your wake-up call.

I didn't write *"ARE YOU READY?"* to entertain you. I wrote it to shake you. To stir something deep inside your spirit that this world has tried to numb. Because whether you realize it or not, time is short, and eternity isn't waiting at your convenience.

Jesus isn't going to text you before He returns. There won't be a countdown or a warning bell. He's coming—suddenly, finally, and forever. And the most important question you'll ever answer isn't "Are you religious?" or "Do you go to church?" It's this: *Are you ready?*

Not halfway. Not casually. Not "I'm a good person" ready.

I'm talking about *heart-on-fire, sin-repenting, eyes-fixed-on-eternity* ready.

This book isn't about self-improvement. It's about surrender. It's about burning away every excuse, every distraction, and every ounce of lukewarm faith that's kept you from going all-in with Jesus. Each chapter was crafted to serve as a match meant to be struck, to set your heart ablaze, and to light the path back to God's purpose for your life.

You may not feel ready now, but that's okay. He's not calling the already prepared. He's calling the willing.

As you read, I pray you'll rediscover (or discover for the first time) the fire you were meant to carry. The boldness you were born for. The urgency your soul has been craving.

God is calling you.

Not to play it safe, but to walk in surrender.
Not to blend in, but to burn bright.
Not to be admired, but to be ablaze.

So flip the page. Don't skim. Don't shrug this off. The Holy Spirit is ready.

Are you?

Let's find out—together.

—T.A. Braddock

Chapter 1: The Silent Drift

"Be on guard, so that your hearts will not be weighed down with dissipation and drunkenness and the worries of life, and that day will not come on you suddenly like a trap..."
— Luke 21:34 (NASB)

Asleep at the Wheel

It doesn't happen all at once. It's slow. Quiet. Easy.

That's how the enemy works.
That's how the drift begins.

One day, you're waking up early, Bible open, heart wide.
You feel God's presence. You hear His voice.
You pray with purpose. You walk in obedience.
And then—
You start hitting snooze.
You skip church one Sunday, then another.
You scroll more than you pray.
You sing worship songs, but don't feel them.
You smile during sermons but haven't repented in years.

You're still a "Christian." You still believe in God.
But something is missing. And you can't remember when it happened.

Friend, this is the silent drift, and it is deadly.

A Warning from Jesus Himself

Jesus didn't whisper about this danger.
He shouted about it over and over again.

In Luke 21, He warned:

"Be on guard... that day will close on you suddenly like a trap."

That "day" is His return. Judgment Day.
The day when every soul will stand before God and give an account.

But He wasn't just warning the lost.
He was warning believers. People like you and me.
People who are busy. Distracted.
Caught in the worries of life.
Numbed by comfort.
Too tired to pray.
Too busy to care.

He was warning us:

Don't fall asleep. Don't drift. Don't let your guard down.

Satan Doesn't Need You to Deny Jesus. Just Forget Him.

The devil's smartest tactic isn't to make you a full-blown atheist.
He just needs you to forget.

Forget how you used to weep during worship.
Forget how you once begged God to use your life.
Forget how Jesus bled on the cross to save your soul.
Forget that time is short and eternity is long.

He doesn't steal your faith in one big moment.
He slowly replaces it with comfort... with distraction... with noise.

He convinces you that a little sin isn't a big deal.
That prayer can wait. That holiness is optional.
That the fire you once had... it's just part of growing older.

No. That's a lie.
You were not saved to sit still.
You were saved to burn.

You Can Be a Christian and Still Be Asleep

Yes, you read that right.
You can believe in Jesus and still be spiritually asleep.

The churches in Revelation were full of people who thought they were alive.
But Jesus said, "You have a name that you're alive, but you are dead." (Revelation 3:1)

They had religion, but no fire.
Church membership, but no repentance.
Knowledge, but no hunger.

Sound familiar?

That's where many of us are today.

We know the songs.
We know the verses.
But we've lost the urgency.
We've lost the fear of God.
We've lost the holy desperation that once drove us to our knees.

A World on Fire and a Church Asleep

Look around you.
The world is on fire.
Chaos is rising.
Truth is being silenced.
Evil is being called good.
And the return of Christ is closer than it's ever been.

And yet...
Many believers are more passionate about their favorite show than their Savior.
More interested in fitness goals than faith.
More offended by political opinions than by sin.
More afraid of cancel culture than of hell.

The church isn't just in danger of drifting.

We're already adrift.

And it's time to wake up.

Wake Up Before It's Too Late

I'm not writing this to scare you.

I'm writing this because I love you.
And Jesus loves you even more.

But love warns.
Love tells the truth.
Love doesn't stay quiet when the house is on fire.

And right now?
The spiritual house is on fire.

If you've been drifting...
If your fire has faded...
If you can't remember the last time you truly repented...
If you can't remember the last time you shared the gospel...
If you've been going through the motions...

Wake. Up. Now.

There may not be another warning.
Another book.
Another sermon.
Another Sunday.

This could be your last chance to get right with God.

It Starts With One Honest Look in the Mirror

Jesus isn't asking you to fix yourself.
He's asking you to come back to Him.

But first, you must be honest.

Where have you compromised?
What sins have you allowed to linger?
What secret doors have you left unlocked?
What idols are stealing your affection?

This chapter is not about shame.
It's about clarity.
It's about truth.
It's about waking up before the door shuts.

The longer you sleep, the harder it is to wake up.

Jesus Is Knocking Right Now

Revelation 3:20 is one of the most misquoted verses in the Bible.

"Behold, I stand at the door and knock…"

Many think this verse is for unbelievers.
But Jesus said it to the church.

He's not knocking on the heart of a sinner.
He's knocking on the door of a church that kicked Him out.

How heartbreaking.

Could that be you?
Could that be your heart?

Have you pushed Jesus out without realizing it?
Have you silenced His voice under the weight of your

schedule?
Have you traded obedience for comfort?

If so, He is still knocking.

But you must open the door.

One Step Back to the Fire

The good news?
You don't need a spiritual resume to come back.
You don't need to fake it.
You don't need to "get it together."

You just need to say,

"Jesus, I've drifted. I want to come home."

That one prayer can crack open the door.

That one confession can wake you up.
That one cry can bring back the fire.

Your Soul Was Made for Urgency

God didn't make you for lukewarm living.
He made you for fire.
For purpose.
For mission.
For love that burns so bright, the world can't ignore it.

But first, you must admit you've drifted.
And ask Him to wake you up.

One Thing to Remember

The most dangerous place to be is spiritually asleep while thinking you're awake.

One Step to Take

Identify one area of spiritual compromise in your life right now. Write it down. Pray over it. Ask God to remove it and reignite your heart.

One Scripture to Read Again

Luke 21:34-36 –

"Be on guard, so that your hearts will not be weighed down with dissipation and drunkenness and the worries of life, and that day will not come on you suddenly like a trap... Keep on the alert at all times."

Chapter 2: The Danger of Lukewarm Faith

"I know your works, that you are neither cold nor hot. I wish you were either one or the other! So because you are lukewarm—neither hot nor cold—I am about to spit you out of My mouth."
— Revelation 3:15-16 (NIV)

The Words No Christian Wants to Hear

Imagine standing before Jesus Christ, the Savior you claimed to follow, the One who gave everything for you.

Imagine looking into His eyes, expecting to hear, "Well done, good and faithful servant."

But instead, He says:

"You made Me sick."

That's what spit you out means.

That's not my opinion. That's not an exaggeration.
Those are His words.

To the church in Laodicea, Jesus gave one of the harshest warnings in all of Scripture, not to atheists or murderers, but to lukewarm believers.

People who looked spiritual on the outside but were dead inside.
People who had just enough faith to look clean, but not enough to obey.
People who thought they were fine, but were making Jesus nauseous.

This isn't a side issue. This is a salvation issue.

The Church That Had Everything Except Fire

Laodicea was rich.
They had influence. Comfort. Prosperity.
If they had Instagram, their lives would've looked perfect.

And they probably thought they were living for God.

But Jesus pulled back the curtain. He saw the truth.
He told them, bluntly:

"You say, 'I am rich; I have acquired wealth and do not need a thing.' But you do not realize that you are wretched, pitiful, poor, blind and naked." (Revelation 3:17)

They thought they were blessed.
But they were spiritually bankrupt.

They thought they were dressed in success.
But they were naked before a holy God.

They thought they were fine.
Jesus was about to vomit.

What Does Lukewarm Faith Look Like Today?

It looks like singing worship songs with no desire to obey them.

It looks like going to church on Sunday but living like the world on Monday.

It looks like posting a Bible verse while watching porn in secret.

It looks like praying before meals but never seeking God's will.

It looks like giving God your leftovers of your time, your money, and your heart.

Lukewarm faith is spiritual halfheartedness.
It's comfortable Christianity.
It's when Jesus is part of your life, but not the center of it.

And Jesus said it makes Him sick.

Hot or Cold—Pick One

Here's what's crazy:
Jesus said He would rather us be cold than lukewarm.

That shocks most people.
You'd think lukewarm is better than cold.
At least lukewarm people go to church, right?
At least they pray sometimes, right?

But Jesus is clear. He'd rather have your heart be cold than fake.

Why?

Because at least when you're cold, you know you're lost.
There's a chance you'll feel your need for Him.
But when you're lukewarm you feel fine.
You're blind to your condition.

And nothing is harder to wake up than someone who thinks they're already awake.

Lukewarm Faith Is a Path to Hell

Let's not sugarcoat this.

Lukewarm faith doesn't save you.

Jesus didn't die to be your backup plan.
He didn't suffer so He could get your scraps.
He didn't rise from the dead so you could give Him one hour a week and ignore Him the rest of the time.

He is either Lord of all or not Lord at all.

This isn't religion. This is reality.

You can have all the Christian language...
You can wear the shirts and know the songs...
You can go on mission trips and lead small groups...

And still hear Him say,

"I never knew you." (Matthew 7:23)

Lukewarm faith is more dangerous than rebellion.
Because it feels safe.
But it's spiritually deadly.

Signs You Might Be Lukewarm

Ask yourself these questions:

Do I only seek God when I'm in trouble?

Do I pray more out of guilt than love?

Do I prioritize my schedule over God's Word?

Do I avoid sharing my faith out of fear of what people think?

Do I say I love Jesus but live how I want?

Do I compare myself to "worse" Christians, so I feel better?

Do I expect God to bless me while I continue in sin?

If you feel convicted, don't push it away. That conviction could be the very mercy of God pulling you out of your drift.

Jesus Loves You Too Much to Leave You Lukewarm

Here's the good news:
Jesus doesn't just spit out lukewarm believers.
He calls them to repent and come back to the fire.

Revelation 3:19 says:

"Those whom I love I rebuke and discipline. So be earnest and repent."

This isn't about shame.
It's about mercy.
God loves you enough to confront you.
He loves you enough to call you out of compromise.
He loves you enough to pull you out of apathy and into fire.

You're not too far gone.
You haven't drifted too far.

But you must respond.

Fire Requires Fuel

If you want to burn for Jesus, you need more than emotions.
You need fuel.

God's Word fuels your mind.

Prayer fuels your spirit.

Repentance fuels your purity.

Community fuels your strength.

Worship fuels your affection.

Lukewarmness happens when you try to live on yesterday's fire.
But fire fades unless it's fed.

Don't settle for smoke when you were made to blaze.

Jesus Is Still Knocking

Jesus didn't abandon the lukewarm church in Laodicea.

He didn't storm off.
He didn't strike them down.

He knocked.

"Behold, I stand at the door and knock…" (Revelation 3:20)

They pushed Him out.
But He stayed near.

He knocked, hoping someone would answer.

He's still doing that now.
To you.
Right here.
Right now.

Will you let Him back in?

Will you open the door and let the fire return?

From Lukewarm to On Fire

This book isn't a guilt trip.
It's a wake-up call.

You weren't created for a safe, lukewarm version of Christianity.

You were created to carry God's glory.
To be filled with His Spirit.
To walk in boldness and holiness and power.

But it starts by admitting you've cooled off.
It starts by letting Jesus light the flame again.

One Thing to Remember

Lukewarm faith is the most dangerous kind, because it looks alive, but it's spiritually dead.

One Step to Take

Rate your spiritual temperature right now from 1 to 10.
1 = ice cold; 10 = burning on fire for Jesus.

Now ask:
What would it take to raise it by one point this week?

Write it down. And take the step.

One Scripture to Read Again

Revelation 3:15–16

"I know your deeds, that you are neither cold nor hot. I wish you were either one or the other! So, because you are lukewarm—neither hot nor cold—I am about to spit you out of My mouth."

Chapter 3: You Were Born for Fire

"You are the light of the world. A city set on a hill cannot be hidden. Neither do people light a lamp and put it under a bowl. Instead, they put it on its stand, and it gives light to everyone in the house."
— Matthew 5:14–15

You Weren't Saved to Sit Still

Somewhere along the way, the fire went out.

Not because you stopped believing in Jesus,
but because you stopped living like He saved you.

You started blending in.
You started keeping your faith quiet.
You told yourself it was humility or maybe wisdom.

But the truth?
You've been hiding your light.

And the longer it stays hidden,
the harder it is to believe you were meant to shine at all.

Friend, hear this clearly:
You weren't saved to sit in silence.
You weren't forgiven to keep your faith private.
You weren't filled with God's Spirit to coast until Heaven.

You were born for fire.

Jesus Didn't Die to Make You Mild

If you read the Gospels, Jesus never once called someone to be lukewarm, passive, or quietly spiritual.

He called fishermen to leave their nets.
He called tax collectors to abandon their riches.
He called religious leaders to repent or walk away.

He never called someone to stay the same.

When Jesus saves you, He sets you apart.
When He fills you, He sets you on fire.

That fire isn't just for your good; it's for the world to see.

"You are the light of the world…"

Not just your family.
Not just your church.
The world.

Which means your life should glow with the presence of God.
It should shine with truth, with love, with courage.
It should burn so brightly that others feel the warmth of
Heaven when they're near you.

A Light That Hides Is a Life That Lies

Let's not twist Jesus' words. He didn't say:

"You might be the light…"

He said:

"You are the light of the world."

If Christ lives in you, then light lives in you.
And light can't help but shine unless it's hidden.

Jesus warned:

"Neither do people light a lamp and put it under a bowl."

Why would anyone light a fire, then hide it?

Why would anyone carry the hope of eternal life, then stay
silent?

Why would anyone hold the cure to spiritual death, then keep it to themselves?

If the devil can't stop your salvation,
he'll settle for silencing your witness.

He'll whisper:

"Don't make things awkward."

"Don't be that person."

"Don't risk the relationship."

"It's not your job to save anyone."

And if you listen long enough,
you'll start to believe that your faith is a private thing.

That your light is optional.

That obedience is extreme.

That comfort is worth more than calling.

But here's the truth:

A hidden light is no light at all.

The World Needs Fire, Not Fog

Our world doesn't need more nice people.
It needs bold people.
Holy people.
Clear people.
On fire people.

People who speak truth even when it's costly.
People who love the unlovable.
People who fear God more than they fear man.

Right now, darkness is growing louder.
Evil is celebrated.

Sin is paraded.
Truth is mocked.

And too many believers are responding by going quiet.

But now is not the time to shrink back.
Now is the time to shine.

Jesus said:

"Let your light shine before others, so that they may see your good deeds and glorify your Father in heaven." (Matthew 5:16)

The purpose of your light isn't to make you look good.
It's to make God look great.

It's not about spotlight. It's about salvation.
It's not about attention. It's about direction.

Your light points people to Jesus.

The Fire Is Already In You

If you've said yes to Jesus—
if you've repented, believed, and been born again—
then the Holy Spirit is already inside you.

You don't need to find the fire.
You already have it.

But just like a campfire, it needs tending.
A fire ignored will die.

The Apostle Paul told Timothy:

"Fan into flame the gift of God…" (2 Timothy 1:6)

In other words, the fire needs air.
It needs fuel.
It needs attention.

Don't wait until you feel it.
Act on what you know is true.

Open your Bible.
Lift your voice in worship.
Speak up in the face of compromise.
Step out in obedience even if your hands shake.

You were born to burn.
Not once. Not just on a youth retreat. Not just at an altar call.
Every single day.

Real Fire Costs Something

If you decide to live on fire for Jesus, you will lose things.

You might lose friends.
You might lose influence.
You might lose comfort.
You might lose control.

But what you gain is worth it all.

You gain peace the world can't steal.
You gain clarity in a world of confusion.
You gain purpose that doesn't die when life gets hard.
And most of all, you gain Christ.

You were not meant for a dim, flickering faith.
You were created for light so bright, it breaks chains.

Stories of Fire

Moses was changed by fire.

A burning bush, not consumed. (Exodus 3)
It turned a stuttering shepherd into a prophet who stood before Pharaoh.

Elijah was vindicated by fire.

Fire fell on Mount Carmel. (1 Kings 18)
It silenced false prophets and turned a nation's heart back to God.

The early church was launched by fire.

Tongues of fire rested on their heads. (Acts 2)
And from that upper room, the gospel exploded across the earth.

And you?

What could God do if you stopped hiding?

What would happen if your life became a flame again?

Let Your Light Speak Louder Than Your Fear

Your light is not just your words. It's your life.

When you forgive when others would hold a grudge…
When you serve when others are selfish…
When you resist temptation…
When you speak truth kindly, even if it's not popular…

You shine.

Your light doesn't have to be loud.
But it must be visible.

You don't have to scream.
You just have to shine.

If You've Been Hiding, You're Not Alone

We've all hidden the light at times.
We've all had moments when we chose silence over obedience.

Peter did.
He denied Jesus three times.

But when Jesus restored him, Peter didn't go back to hiding.

He preached.
He healed.
He suffered.
And he burned so brightly that his enemies said,

"These men have turned the world upside down!" (Acts 17:6)

You don't have to stay in hiding.

Today, Jesus is saying,

"Come out from under the bowl. Let your light shine again."

One Thing to Remember

You weren't saved to survive. You were saved to shine.

One Step to Take

Write down one way you are hiding your light.
It could be fear of what others think, a habit that's dimming
your witness, or a truth you've been too afraid to share.
Then ask Jesus for the courage to step out and shine.

One Scripture to Read Again

Matthew 5:14–16

"You are the light of the world. A city on a hill cannot be
hidden. Neither do people light a lamp and put it under a
bowl. Instead, they put it on its stand, and it gives light to
everyone in the house."

Chapter 4: What If Today Was Your Last Day?

"Why, you do not even know what will happen tomorrow. What is your life? You are a mist that appears for a little while and then vanishes."
— James 4:14

The Call No One Ever Expects

It started like any other day.

He kissed his wife goodbye. He grabbed his keys.
He had plans to stop for coffee, hit the gym, and make it to work early.
He was only 42—healthy, successful, respected.
The kind of man everyone thought would live a long, full life.

But that afternoon, the call came.

Car accident. Drunk driver. Gone on impact.

No warning. No goodbye. No chance to make things right.

Imagine standing at his funeral and watching the faces.
Shock. Grief. Regret.
Some cried because they missed him.
Others cried because they never told him what they needed to say.

And all I could think was:
He had no idea that day would be his last.

The Illusion of More Time

We all assume we have time.

Time to say sorry.
Time to forgive.
Time to obey.
Time to change.
Time to finally get serious about our walk with God.

But James cuts through that illusion with a simple, piercing truth:

"What is your life? You are a mist that appears for a little while and then vanishes." (James 4:14)

A mist.
Not a mountain.
Not an empire.
Not a monument.

A mist.

Here for a moment, gone the next.

Life is short. Eternity is not.

What Would You Do With 24 Hours Left?

Let's be real for a moment.

If you knew you had exactly 24 hours left on earth, what would change?

Would you drop the grudges you've held for years?
Would you finally tell your loved ones you're proud of them?
Would you shut off the TV and open your Bible?
Would you pray like never before?
Would you stop hiding sin and start confessing it?

Would you finally let Jesus have all of you?

The truth is…
The things you would do if you only had 24 hours left
are probably the things you should be doing now.

Because none of us is promised another day.

Tomorrow Is a Lie the Enemy Loves

One of Satan's favorite lies is this:

"You've got time."

He doesn't have to talk you out of following Jesus.
He just has to convince you to do it later.

Later, when life slows down.
Later, when you're done chasing your dreams.
Later, when the kids are grown.
Later, when you've had your fun.

But later isn't guaranteed.
And every "later" pushes your heart a little further from God.

Don't wait until a hospital bed.
Don't wait until the crisis.
Don't wait until it's too late.

Jesus deserves your yes today.

Eternity Is Only One Breath Away

The Bible is clear:

"Each person is destined to die once and after that comes
judgment." (Hebrews 9:27)

Every heartbeat is a countdown.
Every breath is one closer to standing before a holy God.

And on that day, it won't matter…

How many followers you had

How much money you made

How perfect your Instagram looked

How nice your house was

How good of a person people thought you were

What will matter is this:

Did you truly know Jesus?

Did you live for Him or for yourself?

Did your life point others to Him?

Did you obey His Word?

Were you on fire for God or lukewarm and asleep?

You won't get to plead your case.
You won't get to negotiate your record.
You won't get one more day.

What you do now is what counts then.

A Short Life Can Still Be a Bright Light

Jesus lived only 33 years.

John the Baptist's public ministry lasted about one year.

The thief on the cross had minutes and he used them to cry out,

"Jesus, remember me when You come into Your kingdom."

And Jesus answered,

"Today you will be with Me in paradise."

You don't need decades to make an eternal impact.
You need a surrendered heart.

You need a willing spirit.
You need the fire of God burning inside you now.

The time to start shining is not when you're old.
It's not after you retire.
It's not when you feel "ready."

Now is the time.

Stories That Break the Illusion

There was a 14-year-old girl at youth group who raised her hand to receive Christ.
She was shy but said, "I don't want to wait anymore."

That weekend, she was in a tragic boating accident.
She died instantly.

But her name was written in the Lamb's Book of Life.
Because she didn't wait.
She said yes when it mattered most while she still had breath.

I've also known men in their 60s who said,

"I'll get right with God someday."

Some of them never did.
Heart attack. Stroke. Unexpected accident.
They were gone before they ever bowed their knee.

Don't be the one who meant to get right but never did.

Live With Eternity in Mind

C.S. Lewis once said,

"Aim at Heaven and you will get Earth thrown in. Aim at Earth and you will get neither."

Living with eternity in mind doesn't mean you stop living your life.
It means you live with purpose.

You raise your kids with Heaven in mind.
You spend your money with the Kingdom in mind.
You make decisions not just for comfort, but for obedience.
You use your voice not just for opinions, but for the gospel.

You live as if the King is coming back, because He is.

You Have One Life—Spend It Well

Your life is like a match.

You can burn it for yourself, and it will fade into smoke.
Or you can burn it for Jesus, and it will light the way for others.

You don't have time to waste.
You don't have time to play games with sin.
You don't have time to live half-in, half-out.

If you're going to follow Jesus, go all in.

Today might be your last.
Let it count.

One Thing to Remember

You may have plans for tomorrow, but only God knows if you'll get there.

One Step to Take

Journal your answer to this question:
What would I change if I knew I only had 24 hours to live?

Then ask yourself:
Why am I waiting?

One Scripture to Read Again

James 4:14 –

"What is your life? You are a mist that appears for a little while and then vanishes."

Chapter 5: False Peace in a Comfortable Christianity

"And no wonder, for Satan himself masquerades as an angel of light."
— 2 Corinthians 11:14

Numb but Not Noticed

There's a kind of quiet that's not peace.
There's a kind of stillness that's not rest.
There's a kind of calm that's not from God.

It's the numbness of distraction.
The false peace of comfort.
The soul silence of spiritual sleep.

Many Christians today aren't rejecting God outright.
They're just... occupied.

Not with evil.
Not with rebellion.
But with endless comfort.
Endless noise.
Endless scrolling.
Endless "harmless" distractions.

We think we have peace, but it's not peace.
It's anesthesia.

And it's killing our fire.

The Devil's Favorite Disguise

Paul warned us clearly:

"Satan himself masquerades as an angel of light." (2 Corinthians 11:14)

In other words, the enemy doesn't always show up with horns and horror.
He shows up in subtlety.

Sometimes he looks like success.
Or security.
Or entertainment.
Or a full calendar.
Or a busy life.

He doesn't tempt you with destruction.
He tempts you with distraction.

Not because he wants you to crash,
but because he wants you to coast.

If Satan can't destroy your soul,
he'll settle for dimming your light,
numbing your heart,
and keeping you from ever living on fire.

Comfort Is a Slow Poison

The most dangerous thing about comfort isn't the comfort itself.
It's what it replaces.

It replaces hunger.
It replaces urgency.
It replaces dependence.
It replaces passion.

Comfort becomes the new calling.
Ease becomes the goal.
And Jesus becomes an accessory instead of the center.

Before long, you're more excited about a vacation than a revival.

More eager to check social media than seek God.
More interested in Netflix than the presence of the Holy Spirit.

We've traded the upper room for the living room.
We've replaced the altar with the algorithm.

And we wonder why we feel so distant from God.

Noise Is the Enemy of Holiness

If the devil can't make you bad,
he'll make you busy.

Not busy doing evil,
busy doing anything that keeps you from God.

The average Christian spends 2–3 minutes a day in prayer.
But over 3 hours a day on their phone.

Think about that.

What voices are shaping your heart?
What messages are filling your mind?

Every scroll is a sermon.
Every ad is preaching.
Every show is discipling.
Every podcast is forming your worldview.

We're drowning in content
and starving for conviction.

Why You Can't Hear God Anymore

Many people say, "I just don't feel close to God."
Or, "I can't hear His voice like I used to."

The question is: what else are you listening to?

God hasn't gone silent.
But His voice is often quiet.
And it takes space to hear Him.

"Be still, and know that I am God." (Psalm 46:10)

You can't be still when you're always scrolling.
You can't know God when your heart is always numb.

The false peace of a full schedule will make you feel secure,
but it will keep you from ever being set apart.

False Peace Sounds Like This…

"I'm doing fine. Things are going well."

"At least I'm not doing what they're doing."

"I still believe in God. That's enough, right?"

"I'll make time for Him soon. Just not today."

"God understands I'm busy."

These aren't statements of rebellion.
They're statements of lukewarmness.

They sound peaceful—reasonable, even.

But they come from a heart that's been lulled to sleep.

False peace doesn't wake you up.
It rocks you into spiritual complacency.

When the Church Becomes a Sleepy Cruise Instead of a Rescue Ship

The Church was never meant to be a cruise ship.
We weren't called to be entertained, pampered, and fed.

We were called to battle, to rescue, to burn with holy fire.

But modern Christianity has become soft.
Polished. Comfortable. Appealing.
And deeply asleep.

We have padded chairs instead of prayer rooms.
We have lattes instead of lament.
We have feel-good sermons instead of fiery truth.

And Satan applauds.
Because as long as we stay asleep,
we're no threat to him.

Break the Spell

If you're honest, maybe you've felt it too:

That numbness in your spirit.

That lack of urgency.

That dull ache in your soul when you scroll for hours but feel empty inside.

That craving for something real but not knowing where to start.

It's not your phone that's the problem.
It's not your schedule.

It's your soul, trying to breathe.

You don't need another notification.
You need God.

You don't need another podcast.
You need the Word.

You don't need more noise.
You need the presence of the Holy Spirit.

Do a 24-Hour Detox

Let me challenge you right here, right now.

Turn it off.

For just 24 hours:

No phone.

No email.

No social media.

No music unless it leads you to worship.

No Netflix, no games, no endless scrolling.

Turn it all off.

And then… listen.

Go for a walk.
Sit in silence.
Open your Bible.
Pray aloud.
Ask God to speak.

You may be surprised how much you start to feel again.
You may cry.
You may feel anxious at first.
You may even feel restless.

That is your spirit waking up.

Do not push it away. Lean into it.

Real Peace Doesn't Come From Control: It Comes From Christ

Jesus never promised you comfort.
He promised you peace, but only in Him.

"Peace I leave with you; My peace I give you. I do not give to you as the world gives." (John 14:27)

The world gives peace through escape.
Jesus gives peace through presence.

The world offers numbness.
Jesus offers awakening.

The world says, "You're fine. Relax."
Jesus says, "Repent. Return. Wake up."

Which voice will you believe?

One Thing to Remember

The most dangerous thing isn't the enemy's attack. It's the comfort that keeps you from noticing you're asleep.

One Step to Take

Do a 24-hour digital detox.
Turn off the phone.
Cut out the noise.
Get alone with God.
Journal how it feels and what God begins to show you.

One Scripture to Read Again

2 Corinthians 11:14 –

"And no wonder, for Satan himself masquerades as an angel of light."

Chapter 6: The Narrow Road Isn't Crowded

"Enter through the narrow gate. For wide is the gate and broad is the road that leads to destruction, and many enter through it. But small is the gate and narrow the road that leads to life, and only a few find it."
— Matthew 7:13–14 (NIV)

More Doesn't Always Mean Right

We live in a world where crowds equal credibility.
If a restaurant has a long line, it must be good.
If a post goes viral, it must be true.
If a church is packed, it must be right.

But Jesus turns that logic upside down.

He says:

"The road that leads to destruction is broad, and many travel it."
"The road that leads to life is narrow, and few find it."

That should stop every one of us in our tracks.

Jesus didn't say the broad road was evil, scary, or obvious.
He said it was easy to enter and well-traveled.

Most people are on it.

They feel fine. They feel safe.
But they are on the road to hell.

The Broad Road Feels Right Until It Doesn't

Let's be clear. The broad road doesn't always look sinful.
Sometimes it looks polished, professional, and polite.

It's the road of:

"I'm a good person."

"I believe in God, but I'm not religious."

"I just want to be true to myself."

"I don't judge anyone. I just do me."

"As long as you're sincere, that's what matters."

"God knows my heart."

It's the road of half-truths.
The road of compromise.
The road of self over surrender.

And Jesus says that this road leads to destruction.

That's not popular. That's not politically correct.
But it's the truth and truth saves souls.

The Narrow Road Is Hard But It's Holy

Jesus didn't just talk about the narrow road.
He walked it.

He walked it through betrayal.
Through rejection.
Through the Garden of Gethsemane.
Through the cross.

He never promised that the narrow road would be easy.
He said it would be hard.
But He also said it would lead to life.

The narrow road means:

Saying yes to obedience when it costs you something.

Walking away from sin when everyone else stays in it.

Speaking the truth in love, even when it offends.

Forgiving when it would feel better to stay bitter.

Living for the unseen, not the applause of people.

Dying to your flesh every single day.

Few choose this road.
But those who do find life.

Following the Crowd Has Never Led to the Cross

If you find yourself doing what everyone else is doing…
thinking what everyone else is thinking…
believing what culture says is acceptable…

You may not be on the narrow path at all.

You may be walking with the crowd straight toward a cliff.

Jesus never chased the crowd.
He preached sermons that made people leave.
He said hard things. He drew lines. He called people out of comfort and into covenant.

"If anyone would come after Me, he must deny himself, take up his cross daily, and follow Me." (Luke 9:23)

He didn't say, "Follow Me and stay the same."
He said, "Follow Me and die to self."

That's not broad-road preaching.
That's narrow-gate truth.

There Is No Middle Road

Let's settle this now:

There is no third option.
No "medium" road.
No "balanced blend" of broad and narrow.

You are either walking the wide path that leads to destruction, or the narrow one that leads to life.

There is no in-between.

Jesus said in Matthew 12:30,

"Whoever is not with Me is against Me."

You're not measured by how many verses you know.
Or how many years you've been in church.
Or how spiritual your posts look.

You're measured by your direction.

Are you walking toward Christ,
or coasting away from Him?

The Narrow Road Is Less About Perfection, More About Pursuit

Let me be clear. Walking the narrow road doesn't mean you never stumble.
It doesn't mean you never fail or fall.

It means you keep pursuing Jesus when you do.

It means when you sin, you repent.
When you fall, you get back up.
When you feel dry, you seek His face.

The narrow road isn't just about what you avoid. It's about who you follow.

Are you following the Shepherd,
or following the crowd?

Are you letting His voice lead you,
or letting culture shape you?

Every step you take reveals the path you're on.

What the Narrow Road Looks Like in Real Life

Let's paint a picture.

You feel tempted to flirt with that person who isn't your spouse. The broad road says, "It's harmless." The narrow road says, "Run from temptation."

You feel pressure to stay quiet about your faith. The broad road says, "Blend in." The narrow road says, "Be a light."

Your friends joke about sin. The broad road laughs along. The narrow road walks away.

You feel God calling you to give something up—a habit, a relationship, a secret. The broad road says, "You don't have to go that far." The narrow road says, "Lay it down."

Every choice is a step.
Every step reveals your path.
And few are on the path that leads to life.

It's Not Too Late to Turn Around

Maybe you've realized…
You've been walking the broad road.
You've been following the crowd.
You've been choosing comfort over conviction.

The good news?

Jesus didn't close the gate behind Him.

The narrow road is still open.
The invitation is still extended.
The Savior still says,

"Follow Me."

But the path is narrow.

You can't bring your sin.
You can't carry your pride.
You can't drag your idols.

You come low.
You come honest.
You come surrendered.

And when you do,
you find that narrow road isn't empty.

Jesus walks it with you.

One Thing to Remember

The broad road feels safe because it's full.
But the narrow road leads to life and Jesus is waiting there.

One Step to Take

Take time to reflect:

Are you walking the broad path or the narrow one?

Write down two habits, relationships, or beliefs that reveal your path.

Then ask God for the courage to step toward Him, even if it means walking alone.

One Scripture to Read Again

Matthew 7:13–14

"Enter through the narrow gate. For wide is the gate and broad is the road that leads to destruction, and many enter through it. But small is the gate and narrow the road that leads to life, and only a few find it."

Chapter 7: The Gift of Godly Sorrow

"Godly sorrow brings repentance that leads to salvation and leaves no regret, but worldly sorrow brings death."
— 2 Corinthians 7:10 (NIV)

When Conviction Feels Like a Weight But Saves Like a Lifeline

Have you ever been suddenly overwhelmed with the feeling, "I'm not where I should be with God"?

Not guilt because you got caught.
Not shame because someone exposed your sin.
But a deep, personal, holy sorrow that rises up from your soul.

That's not weakness.
That's not condemnation.
That's not God trying to crush you.

That's grace.

That sorrow you feel when you finally realize you've been far from God…
that ache, that pull, that brokenness inside you…

It's not meant to bury you.
It's meant to wake you up.

Godly sorrow is the gift that opens the door to freedom.

Worldly Sorrow vs. Godly Sorrow

There's a big difference between guilt and godly sorrow.

Worldly sorrow is selfish.
It says, "I feel bad I got caught."
"I feel embarrassed."

"I feel like a failure."
It focuses on image, and not on relationship.

Godly sorrow is different.
It says, "I've sinned against God."
"I've grieved the One who loves me most."
"I want to turn around and come home."

Worldly sorrow leads to regret, bitterness, and shame.
Godly sorrow leads to repentance, healing, and joy.

Paul makes it clear in 2 Corinthians 7:10:

"Godly sorrow brings repentance that leads to salvation and leaves no regret…"

No regret.
No chains.
No punishment.
Just grace.

Real Repentance Isn't Tears, It's a Turnaround

We've all had moments where we cried over our sin.
But crying isn't the goal. Changing is the goal.

Repentance isn't just saying sorry.
It's turning around.

In the original language, the word "repent" means to "change your mind"…
to see sin the way God sees it,
to agree with His truth,
and to choose to walk a different way.

It's not cleaning yourself up.
It's not earning forgiveness.
It's not working harder to be good.

It's surrender.

It's laying your sin at the feet of Jesus and saying,

"I don't want this anymore. I want You."

A Story of Two Sorrows

Think about Peter and Judas.

Both failed Jesus.
Both betrayed Him in different ways.
But their sorrow took them in opposite directions.

Judas felt shame. He tried to fix it on his own.
He returned the money. He wept bitterly.
And then he gave up. He chose death.

Peter also wept bitterly. He was heartbroken.
But when Jesus rose, Peter came back.
He let Jesus restore him.
He accepted grace.
And he became a pillar of the Church.

Same failure.
Same sorrow.
Different response.
Different ending.

God doesn't want you to stay in shame.
He wants to redeem your story like Peter.

The Sin You Cover Will Eventually Crush You

Maybe you've been hiding something.

That thought.
That habit.
That compromise no one else knows about.

You've covered it.
Justified it.
Ignored it.

But sin never stays small.
It grows. It spreads. It steals.

The longer you hide it,
the harder your heart becomes.

But here's the truth:
What you cover, God will expose.
What you confess, God will cleanse.

"He who conceals his sins does not prosper, but whoever confesses and renounces them finds mercy." (Proverbs 28:13)

You don't have to carry it anymore.
You don't have to fake it.
You don't have to protect your image.

You can be free, but you have to come clean.

God Isn't Mad, He's Waiting

We often imagine God with arms crossed,
foot tapping,
waiting to unleash punishment.

That's not the heart of the Father.

Look at Luke 15 and the story of the prodigal son.

The boy ran far.
Wasted everything.
Ended up in filth.

But when he came home broken, filthy, and ashamed,
his father didn't rebuke him.

He ran to him.
Threw his arms around him.
Put a robe on his shoulders and a ring on his finger.
He said, "My son was lost, but now he's home."

That's the Father's heart for you.

He's not waiting to punish you.
He's waiting to restore you.

Repentance Isn't a One-Time Event, It's a Way of Life

Some people treat repentance like it's just for the beginning of the Christian life.

They say, "I repented when I got saved."
And that's good.

But repentance isn't just the door to salvation.
It's the path of discipleship.

Repentance is how we stay clean.
It's how we stay close.
It's how we stay soft-hearted in a hard world.

When you sin, repent.
When you drift, repent.
When you feel cold, repent.

Don't run.
Don't numb it.
Don't explain it away.

Just come back.

Over and over again.
Until the day you see Jesus face to face.

Freedom Always Follows Honesty

Some of the most powerful breakthroughs in your life will begin with the most painful moments of honesty.

When you finally say,

"God, I've been prideful."
"I've been addicted."
"I've been jealous."
"I've been disobedient."
"I've loved other things more than You."

It feels like death.
But it leads to resurrection.

Because you can't have freedom without truth.

"Then you will know the truth, and the truth will set you free." (John 8:32)

You don't need to hide anymore.
You don't need to manage your image.
You need to be honest with God.

Repentance Isn't Shame, It's a Shower

Think of repentance like a hot shower after days of dirt.
You don't dread it, you need it.

It washes off the filth.
It clears your mind.
It revives your strength.

That's what godly sorrow does.
It brings you back to the place where you can finally breathe again.

Don't confuse conviction with condemnation.
Conviction says, "There's sin, but also a way out."
Condemnation says, "There's sin, and you're stuck in it."

Conviction is the voice of the Holy Spirit calling you home.
And He never speaks without offering hope.

Are You Ready to Come Clean?

This chapter isn't just about information.
It's an invitation.

To come home.
To come clean.
To come back to the fire.

And it starts with one honest prayer.

One Thing to Remember

True repentance isn't God shaming you—it's Him saving you.

One Step to Take

Write a prayer of honest repentance.
Tell God the truth.
Hold nothing back.
Let it be raw, real, and unfiltered.

Then ask Him to fill the places you once filled with sin.

One Scripture to Read Again

2 Corinthians 7:10 –

"Godly sorrow brings repentance that leads to salvation and leaves no regret, but worldly sorrow brings death."

Chapter 8: When You Finally Say, 'I Surrender All'

"Therefore, I urge you, brothers and sisters, in view of God's mercy, to offer your bodies as a living sacrifice, holy and pleasing to God—this is your true and proper worship."
— Romans 12:1 (NIV)

Surrender Isn't Just for Singers, It's for Soldiers

You've heard the song:

"All to Jesus, I surrender. All to Him I freely give."

We sing it with lifted hands and full hearts.
But what happens when the music stops?
What happens when surrender becomes more than a song?
What happens when it becomes a choice, a command, a cross?

Real surrender has nothing to do with feelings.
It's not about goosebumps.
It's not about tears in a church pew.

It's about giving God everything: no conditions, no backup plans, no turning back.

Jesus Doesn't Want a Slice, He Wants the Whole Pie

Some of us treat our lives like a pie chart.

One slice for work.

One slice for family.

One slice for hobbies.

One slice for God usually on Sundays.

But Jesus doesn't want to be part of your life.
He wants to own it.

"Offer your bodies as a living sacrifice..." (Romans 12:1)

That's not a casual request. That's a command.

Jesus gave His whole body for you:
nailed to a cross, blood pouring, heart breaking.

And He asks for yours in return.

Not just your time. Not just your money.
Your whole self.

Living Sacrifice Means You Don't Get Off the Altar

Paul didn't say, "Offer your lives for a few minutes."
He said, "Offer your bodies as living sacrifices."

That means every day, every hour, every part of you is
surrendered to God.

Your mouth is what you say.

Your eyes are what you look at.

Your ears are what you listen to.

Your hands are what you touch and build.

Your feet are where you go.

Your mind is what you think about.

Your heart is what you desire most.

Nothing held back.
No rooms left locked.
No sins kept for "just one more time."

Everything on the altar.

The Illusion of Control Must Die

Let's be honest.

We like the idea of surrender until God actually asks for control.
We want to follow Jesus but still make our own plans.
We want the crown but skip the cross.

But true surrender means giving up control.
It means saying:

"God, You can have my relationships."

"God, You can have my dreams."

"God, You can have my money."

"God, You can have my reputation."

"God, You can have my future."

Even if it costs me everything, You're worth it.

That's not weakness. That's worship.

The Rich Young Ruler Walked Away Full But Empty

In Mark 10, a wealthy young man ran up to Jesus and asked what he needed to do to inherit eternal life.

He had kept the commandments.
He lived clean.
He looked the part.

But Jesus saw the idol in his heart.

"Go, sell all you have, give to the poor, and follow Me."

The man's face fell.
He turned around.
And he walked away not because he didn't believe,
but because he wouldn't surrender.

How many of us are doing the same?

Still near Jesus.
Still in church.
Still saying all the right things.
But still holding back.

The Danger of Almost Surrendered

Almost surrendered means:

You give God your sin, but not your schedule.

You give Him your words, but not your thought life.

You give Him Sundays, but not your decisions.

You give Him the big stuff, but keep control of the daily stuff.

Almost surrendered is still disobedience.

God doesn't want part of your heart.
He wants the whole thing.

Not because He's a control freak.
Because He knows that life only works when He's first.

Real Surrender Sets You Free

You might think surrender sounds like losing.

In the world's eyes, it is.

But in the Kingdom, surrender is where freedom begins.

When you let go of control,
you gain peace.

When you stop chasing your own dreams,
you gain purpose.

When you give up your rights,
you receive power.

And when you die to yourself,
you truly begin to live.

"Whoever loses his life for My sake will find it." (Matthew 10:39)

This is upside-down truth.
It's cross-shaped wisdom.
It's the only path to fire-filled, Spirit-led living.

Your Surrender List

Let's get practical.

What are you still holding back from God?

Is it your phone habits?

A relationship that's unhealthy?

A secret sin no one knows about?

A career you won't let Him touch?

A wound you won't let Him heal?

Make a list. Seriously.

Write down everything you haven't truly placed on the altar.

Then do something brave and pray through it.

Lay each one at His feet.
Out loud.
One by one.

And say, "I surrender this to You."

Don't just read this chapter. Respond to it.

What Happens When You Really Let Go

When you finally surrender…

Your prayer life becomes intimate.

The Bible comes alive.

Worship becomes real.

Sin loses its grip.

Fear loses its power.

You stop needing the world's approval.

You start living with confidence and joy.

That's the fruit of surrender.

And it starts the moment you stop fighting God and simply say:
"Yes, Lord."

The Fire Falls on the Altar

In the Old Testament, the fire of God didn't fall on the people. It fell on the altar.

It consumed the sacrifice.

If you want God's fire—His power, His presence, His revival—
then you need to build an altar in your heart.

And place your whole life on it.

No reservations.
No bargaining.
No escape clause.

Just a total, honest, humble surrender.

That's where the fire falls.

One Thing to Remember

Surrender isn't losing. It's gaining the life you were created for.

One Step to Take

Make a "Surrender List."
Write down every area of your life you've been holding back.
Then pray through it.
Say out loud: "God, I give You this."
Ask Him to take control and fill you with His power and peace.

One Scripture to Read Again

Romans 12:1 –

"Therefore, I urge you, brothers and sisters, in view of God's mercy, to offer your bodies as a living sacrifice, holy and pleasing to God—this is your true and proper worship."

Chapter 9: Break the Chains You Forgot You Were Wearing

"Jesus replied, 'Very truly I tell you, everyone who sins is a slave to sin... But if the Son sets you free, you will be free indeed.'"
— John 8:34–36 (NIV)

When Chains Start to Feel Normal

Have you ever worn a heavy backpack for so long,
you stopped noticing the weight?

At first, it's uncomfortable.
But over time, your body adjusts.
The pressure doesn't disappear. You just stop feeling it.

That's how sin works.

At first, it stings.
It pricks your conscience.
It keeps you up at night.

But if you ignore it long enough,
you start to forget it's even there.

You call it "just a habit."
"Just a part of who I am."
"Not that big of a deal."

But what feels normal can still be a chain.

And chains are meant to be broken.

Sin Doesn't Start as a Prison

No one plans to become a slave to sin.

It always starts small.
A click.
A compromise.
A secret.
A shortcut.

At first, you feel in control.

You tell yourself,

"I can stop whenever I want."

But slowly, quietly, that sin begins to wrap itself around you.

What began as a choice becomes a habit.
What began as a temptation becomes a lifestyle.
What began as a whisper becomes a stronghold.

Before you know it, you're stuck.

You try to stop.
You promise to change.
You cry at the altar.
But the chain holds.

Why?

Because sin doesn't just stain you, it enslaves you.

"Everyone who sins is a slave to sin…" (John 8:34)

The Devil Doesn't Need to Destroy You Just to Bind You

The enemy's goal isn't always destruction in one day.
He's more patient than that.

He'll settle for slow spiritual paralysis.

He just wants to:

Weaken your resolve

Dull your passion

Steal your joy

Rob your testimony

Keep you "saved" but silent

And the most effective way he does it?

Unconfessed, unchallenged sin.

He'll let you go to church.
He'll let you read your Bible.
He'll even let you serve,
as long as you keep that one habit, that one addiction, that one secret.

Because that's the chain that keeps you from running free.

Sin Desensitizes Before It Destroys

When sin first enters your life, it shocks you.
But over time, it numbs you.

You stop feeling conviction.
You stop hearing the Holy Spirit.
You stop seeing the need to change.

And that's exactly what the enemy wants.

If Satan can't destroy you,
he'll deaden you.

He wants your fire to fade.
Your boldness to shrink.
Your light to dim.

And it all begins with a chain you stopped noticing.

The Light Reveals What the Dark Tries to Hide

The most dangerous sins are the ones we keep in the dark.

They grow stronger in secrecy.
They thrive in silence.
They feed off your shame.

But the moment you bring them into the light,
they begin to lose their power.

"But everything exposed by the light becomes visible—and everything that is illuminated becomes a light." (Ephesians 5:13)

Confession doesn't make you weak.
It makes you free.

You don't have to tell the whole world.
But you do need to tell God, and often someone you trust.

Because what stays hidden stays powerful.
But what you expose, God can heal.

Jesus Didn't Come to Make You a Better Slave, He Came to Set You Free

Some people think being a Christian means just learning to "manage" their sin.

They accept a low level of bondage.
They convince themselves,

"I'll always struggle with this."
"This is just who I am."

No.

Jesus didn't come to make you a little less broken.
He came to make you brand new.

"If the Son sets you free, you will be free indeed." (John 8:36)

Not halfway free.
Not "kinda" free.
Free indeed.

That means the chain can break.
The shame can lift.
The cycle can end.

But you have to be willing to admit:

"I'm not free yet, but I want to be."

Name Your Chain

Right now, you probably know what it is.

That one habit.

That one secret.

That one thought pattern.

That one thing you keep going back to.

It may not be obvious to the world.
But it's holding you back.

You've convinced yourself it's manageable.
But deep down, you know it's not.

It's slowing you down.
It's stealing your joy.
It's silencing your voice.
It's making you live half-awake.

So here's the question:

Are you ready to break it?

What Freedom Requires

Freedom is not found in willpower.

It's found in surrender.

If you could break the chain yourself,
you would have done it already.

But Jesus didn't ask you to fight sin alone.
He asks you to give Him the chain.

He asks you to:

Admit your need

Confess your sin

Invite His Spirit to change you

Walk in community

Stay close to His Word

Replace lies with truth

Resist the enemy daily

Freedom isn't always instant.
Sometimes it's a fight.
Sometimes it's a process.
But the power is always available when Jesus is Lord.

A Word for the Weary

Maybe you've been trying for years.
You've asked for freedom before.
You've repented. You've prayed. You've cried.

But you keep falling.

Listen to me carefully:

Don't quit.

Your past doesn't define you.
Your struggle doesn't disqualify you.
Your failure isn't final.

God's mercy is new this morning.
And His power is enough.

One day, the chain that feels unbreakable
will snap like a twig in the hands of Jesus.

Just don't give up.

The Fire Falls Where Chains Are Broken

When the early church experienced revival in Acts 19,
they brought out their scrolls of sorcery worth millions and
burned them in public.

Why?

Because when you get serious about Jesus,
you get serious about breaking free.

And when chains break, fire falls.

If you want God to move in power,
you've got to walk in purity.

Freedom isn't for the perfect.
It's for the humble.

It's for those who say,

"Jesus, I don't want to live this way anymore.
I'm tired of carrying this chain.
I want to be free."

That prayer?
That's where the fire begins.

One Thing to Remember

What you tolerate in secret will eventually take control in public.
Bring the chain into the light and let Jesus break it.

One Step to Take

Identify one hidden habit, thought, or pattern that's holding you back.
Write it down.
Confess it to God and to someone you trust.
Ask for prayer.
Take one bold step this week to cut it off and walk free.

One Scripture to Read Again

John 8:34–36

"Very truly I tell you, everyone who sins is a slave to sin... But if the Son sets you free, you will be free indeed."

Chapter 10: Burn the Backup Plan

"Jesus replied, 'No one who puts a hand to the plow and looks back is fit for service in the kingdom of God.'"
— Luke 9:62 (NIV)

The Exit Door You Pretend You'll Never Use

You say you've given your life to Jesus.
You sing, you serve, you show up.

But if you're honest…
You've still got a backup plan.

That "just in case" door.
That little space you've kept untouched.
That safety net if obedience gets uncomfortable.

Maybe it's a secret habit.
Maybe it's a relationship you haven't let go of.
Maybe it's the old life you keep visiting in your mind.
Maybe it's an idol you say you've laid down, but you're still holding the leash.

You tell God,

"Yes, Lord… but not that."
"Yes, Lord… unless it costs this much."
"Yes, Lord… as long as I still get this part of my life."

But Jesus didn't call us to live for Him with conditions.

He called us to burn the backup plan.

You Can't Move Forward While Looking Back

Jesus didn't mince words:

"No one who puts his hand to the plow and looks back is fit for service in the kingdom of God." (Luke 9:62)

He wasn't being dramatic.
He was being clear.

You can't walk in power while clinging to your past.
You can't live on fire while planning your escape.
You can't say "Yes" and "Maybe" to Jesus in the same breath.

Looking back divides your heart.
It weakens your focus.
It steals your joy.
And it puts your obedience on pause.

The plow only works if you face forward.

Faith Doesn't Keep a Safety Net

Imagine if Noah had said,

"I'll build the ark, but I'm also digging a cave just in case."

Imagine if Peter had said,

"I'll walk on water, but let me tie a rope to the boat just in case."

Imagine if Jesus had said,

"I'll go to the cross, but keep the angels on standby just in case."

They didn't.
Because faith doesn't need a "just in case."
It needs full surrender.

You can't walk by faith while leaning on your own backup plans.

Burn the Boats: The Story of No Return

In the 1500s, Hernán Cortés sailed from Spain to Mexico with a fleet of ships and a small army.

When they landed on the shore, he gave an order that shocked everyone:

"Burn the boats."

No retreat. No turning back. No safety plan.

And from that moment forward, they knew, we either move forward or we die.

Now listen: we don't honor Cortés for his cause.
But we can't ignore his commitment.

What if you had the same attitude toward your walk with Christ?

What if you burned the boats?
What if you removed the exit signs?
What if you let go of every "just in case" and said,

"Jesus, there is no plan B. I'm all in."

The Lie of the 'Secret Option'

Satan will try to convince you that it's smart to keep your options open.

"Don't be extreme."
"Just play it safe."
"You never know what the future holds."
"You might regret giving this up."

But here's what the enemy won't tell you:

Your backup plan is your bondage.

That secret option?

It's keeping you double-minded.

It's slowing down your obedience.

It's giving the enemy a foothold.

It's whispering, "You don't have to trust God all the way."

Half-hearted obedience is still disobedience.

The Cost of Keeping Your Options Open

Let's talk real life.

If God tells you to give, do you hesitate thinking about what you'll miss?
If God tells you to forgive, do you keep the bitterness "just in case" you need it later?
If God tells you to speak truth, do you hold back, worried about losing approval?

That's a backup plan.

And as long as it's there, you'll never walk in full authority.

You'll always second-guess.
You'll always be unstable.
You'll always wonder why your fire won't last.

"A double-minded man is unstable in all his ways." (James 1:8)

The fire of God doesn't fall on people with exit strategies.

It falls on the ones who say,

"If I perish, I perish. But I'm not turning back."

There's Power in Burning the Bridge

Think of Elisha.

When Elijah called him to follow, Elisha didn't hesitate.
He slaughtered his oxen, burned the plows, and followed the prophet.

He didn't say,

"Let me hold onto this in case the prophet thing doesn't work out."

No. He burned his Plan B.

And from that moment forward, Elisha walked in power.

He didn't have a backup plan. He had obedience.

What's the plow in your life that still ties you to the old you?

A toxic relationship?

An addiction you refuse to confront?

A job or calling God's asked you to release?

A dream you're chasing more than Jesus?

You won't see God's fullness until you burn the thing you keep just in case He doesn't come through.

God Can't Fill What You Won't Empty

If your hands are full of backup plans,
they're too full to carry His presence.

If your heart is full of compromise,
there's no room for fire.

God doesn't bless halfway faith.
He responds to total surrender.

"Trust in the Lord with all your heart and lean not on your own understanding…" (Proverbs 3:5)

It doesn't say "with most of your heart."
It says all.

You either lean on His Word or your backup plan.
You can't do both.

Let Go of the Lifeboat

Maybe your lifeboat isn't sin.
Maybe it's fear.
Maybe it's a version of control you've clung to for years.

But God is calling you out of the boat and onto the water.
Not because it's safe,
but because it's where He is.

And the only way to walk in supernatural freedom
is to step out, leave the backup plan behind,
and say:

"Even if I fall, I'd rather fall in faith than survive in fear."

You'll Never Regret Going All In

No one in Heaven will say,

"I wish I'd held more back from God."
"I wish I'd played it safer."
"I wish I'd followed Jesus halfway."

But there will be people who look back in eternity and say:

"I was almost surrendered."
"I almost obeyed."
"I almost went all in."

Don't be almost.

Don't live with half-hearted fire.
Don't carry the weight of a Plan B faith.

Burn the backup plan.
And step into the power of total surrender.

One Thing to Remember

You can't follow Jesus fully while holding on to your escape route.

One Step to Take

Ask yourself:
What's your backup plan to disobey God?
That thing you're still keeping in your back pocket "just in case"?

Write it down. Name it.
Then let it go.
Pray out loud: "Jesus, I give this up. I choose obedience. There is no plan B."

One Scripture to Read Again

Luke 9:62 –

"No one who puts a hand to the plow and looks back is fit for service in the kingdom of God."

Chapter 11: Deliverance Starts with a Decision

"And these signs will accompany those who believe: In My name they will drive out demons..."
— Mark 16:17 (NIV)

Freedom Isn't for the Special—It's for the Surrendered

Some people think deliverance is only for the deeply broken.
The addicts. The possessed. The hopeless.

But the truth is, every believer needs deliverance at some point.
Not just once, but often.
Because we live in a fallen world,
and the enemy doesn't stop just because we said a prayer.

Jesus didn't say deliverance was optional.
He said it was normal.

"These signs will follow those who believe..."
Not pastors.
Not preachers.
Not super-Christians.

Those who believe.

That means you.

The Authority You Forgot You Had

You don't need to be a prophet to cast down strongholds.
You don't need a microphone to walk in spiritual authority.
You just need to know who you are in Christ.

If you belong to Jesus,
you have the Spirit of the Living God inside of you.

That means:

You don't have to stay bound.

You don't have to live afraid.

You don't have to beg for freedom.

You don't have to tolerate darkness in your life.

You are a blood-bought, Spirit-filled, heaven-backed child of God.
And that means you can stand up and say no to every lie, addiction, fear, or bondage.

Deliverance is not about screaming louder.
It's about standing firmer.

It's not about your strength.
It's about your legal right as a son or daughter of God.

Your Words Are a Weapon

The Bible says life and death are in the power of the tongue. (See Proverbs 18:21)

That means when you speak in the name of Jesus,
things move.

Chains break.
Lies lose power.
Fear starts to shrink.
Demons tremble.

"They overcame him by the blood of the Lamb and the word of their testimony…" (Revelation 12:11)

Your mouth matters.
What you say out loud has weight in the spiritual world.

That's why this chapter has an action step you must do out loud:

"I break agreement with ___ in Jesus' name."

Fill in the blank.
Call it by name.

Fear

Lust

Pride

Bitterness

Shame

Control

Anger

Addiction

Insecurity

People-pleasing

A specific sin or pattern

If you don't break the agreement, the enemy will assume you're still in contract.

Every Chain Begins with an Agreement

Spiritual chains don't just appear.
They are formed through agreements.

You may not have realized you signed anything.
But every time you say "yes" to a lie,
you're saying "no" to the truth.

That's agreement.

Believing "I'll never be free" is an agreement.

Thinking "This is just who I am" is an agreement.

Saying "I'll never change" is an agreement.

Holding onto bitterness is an agreement.

Justifying sin is an agreement.

But here's the good news:

What you agreed with in darkness,
you can break in the light.

And all it takes is a decision: a holy, heaven-backed, Spirit-filled declaration of war.

Deliverance Is a Doorway, Not a Detour

Deliverance isn't some extra-credit thing for extreme cases. It's part of your walk with Christ.

The moment you said yes to Jesus,
you stepped into a battle between kingdoms.

You left the kingdom of darkness.
But now, you have to enforce that transfer.

That means you:

Renounce sin

Break ties with anything demonic

Choose obedience

Speak truth

Walk in the light

Reject every stronghold

Declare freedom in Jesus' name

This isn't about chasing demons.
It's about refusing to let them stay.

You don't need to fear the devil.
He needs to fear you when you know your authority.

Deliverance Doesn't Always Feel Dramatic

Movies show people shaking, screaming, and flailing around.
But real deliverance often looks like:

A quiet moment of conviction

A whispered prayer of repentance

A tear-streaked surrender in your room

A choice to cancel a toxic relationship

A word spoken out loud in faith

A decision to finally bring something into the light

And sometimes there is resistance.
The enemy hates to lose ground.
But his power is nothing compared to the authority of the
One who lives in you.

Deliverance isn't about how loud you pray.
It's about who you're praying in.

"In My name..." Jesus said. That's the key.

Your Freedom Is Waiting on Your Decision

You don't have to live bound.
But you do have to decide.

Decide that fear won't control your mind anymore.

Decide that lust won't pollute your soul anymore.

Decide that compromise won't shape your walk anymore.

Decide that you will not live another day in chains.

Speak it.
Mean it.
Stand on it.

"I break agreement with __ in Jesus' name."

Don't wait until you "feel ready."
You're ready when you decide.

Deliverance Leads to Devotion

Freedom isn't just about what you leave behind,
it's about who you run toward.

When the chains fall off, don't walk away empty.
Run to Jesus.
Worship.
Fill your mind with Scripture.
Surround yourself with truth.
Stay in the light.

"When an impure spirit comes out... it returns to find the house empty." (Matthew 12:43–45)

Don't just clean the house. Fill it.

With prayer.
With purity.
With praise.
With the power of God.

Freedom is the beginning not the end.

Today Can Be the Day Everything Changes

You don't have to wait for a Sunday service.
You don't have to wait for a preacher to lay hands on you.
You don't need a stage, a spotlight, or a conference.

You need a decision.

Right here. Right now.

"Jesus, I want to be free.
I break agreement with this lie, this sin, this stronghold.
I renounce it in Your name.
Fill me with Your Spirit.
I receive Your freedom.
I am Yours. Amen."

That may not sound like much to others.
But in the spirit world, chains just shattered.

One Thing to Remember

Freedom doesn't wait for a feeling. It begins with a decision—and your words carry weight in the Spirit.

One Step to Take

Speak this out loud:

"In the name of Jesus, I break agreement with _____. I renounce it. I no longer belong to fear (or whatever you named). I belong to Jesus. I am free, and I walk in His power."

Then follow it up with a time of worship. Thank God for your freedom.

One Scripture to Read Again

Mark 16:17 –

"And these signs will accompany those who believe: In My name they will drive out demons…"

Chapter 12: Let the Holy Spirit Clean You Out

"He saved us, not because of righteous things we had done, but because of His mercy. He washed us through the rebirth and renewal by the Holy Spirit."
— Titus 3:5 (NIV)

Your Soul Is a House: Is It Ready for God to Move In?

Imagine someone coming to stay at your home.
Not a guest.
Not a visitor.

Someone who moves in. Lives there. Shares the space.

You wouldn't leave the dishes piled up.
You wouldn't let the trash overflow.
You wouldn't hide mold in the corners and pretend it doesn't stink.

You'd clean.

Not to impress, but to prepare.

Now imagine this:
The Holy Spirit is not a visitor in your life.
He's not dropping by on Sunday mornings.
He dwells in you.

"Do you not know that your body is a temple of the Holy Spirit?" (1 Corinthians 6:19)

If He's going to live there,
the house needs to be clean.

Not perfect.
Not polished.
But surrendered and ready to be purified.

The Holy Spirit Doesn't Just Comfort: He Cleans

Many people think of the Holy Spirit as the One who brings peace,
goosebumps, encouragement, or a warm feeling during worship.

That's true.

But He is so much more.

The Holy Spirit is the fire of God.
And fire purifies.

"He will baptize you with the Holy Spirit and fire." (Matthew 3:11)

He doesn't come just to comfort you.
He comes to clean you out.

He convicts.
He exposes.
He uproots.
He confronts.

Not to condemn you,
but to refine you.

His Mercy Washes, But His Fire Refines

Titus 3:5 says we are saved not because we're good,
but because He is merciful.

He washes us.
He renews us.
He gives us a fresh start by the Holy Spirit.

But here's what many miss:

The Holy Spirit doesn't just rinse you.
He goes deeper.

He purifies the parts of you that you've ignored for years.

That root of bitterness you buried under "I'm fine."

That pride you've dressed up as confidence.

That secret compromise you've excused again and again.

That unforgiveness you don't want to touch.

That fear you've called wisdom.

He sees it all.
And He wants to clean it out.

Let Him Open Every Door

Imagine your soul like a house with many rooms.

Some rooms are clean.
Some rooms are messy.
Some rooms are locked, and you haven't let anyone in for years.

The Holy Spirit walks through the front door with gentleness and power.

He doesn't barge in.
He knocks.
He waits.

"Behold, I stand at the door and knock..." (Revelation 3:20)

But when you open the door,
He starts cleaning.

And here's the question:

Will you let Him into every room?

Not just the ones that feel spiritual.
Not just the rooms you've already cleaned up.
But the attics of bitterness, the basements of fear, the closets
of compromise.

If you let Him in,
He'll do what no self-help, no sermon, no strategy can do.

He'll make you clean from the inside out.

Purifying Fire Doesn't Destroy: It Transforms

When you hear the word "fire," maybe you flinch.

You think pain. Loss. Judgment.

But the fire of the Holy Spirit isn't for destruction.
It's for refinement.

"He will sit as a refiner and purifier of silver…" (Malachi 3:3)

When silver is refined, the heat rises
and the impurities come to the surface.

That's what the Holy Spirit does.

He allows pressure.
He allows discomfort.
He turns up the heat not to punish you,
but to bring what's hidden to the top so it can be removed.

Don't fear the fire.
Welcome it.

Because what remains after the fire
is pure.
Solid.
Ready.

Stop Cleaning Yourself: Invite Him to Do It

Some people spend years trying to clean themselves up.

They pray harder.
They try harder.
They keep failing and they live in shame.

But the Holy Spirit doesn't need your effort.
He needs your permission.

"Holy Spirit, search me. Clean me. Fill me."

That one prayer invites the cleansing fire of God.

You don't need to be afraid.
He knows what's in you already.

You're not surprising Him.
You're surrendering to Him.

Invite Him In: Room by Room

Here's how it works:

1. Ask Him to search your heart.
Like David prayed in Psalm 139:

"Search me, God, and know my heart; test me and know my anxious thoughts."

2. Be still. Let Him speak.
You may feel something. You may remember something.
Let Him bring it up.

3. Don't argue. Don't justify.
Just say, "Yes, Lord. That's real. That's me. I give it to You."

4. Ask Him to cleanse you.
He is faithful to do it.

5. Thank Him and stay open.
This is not a one-time moment.
It's a way of life.

The Clean Heart Is the Ready Heart

You want to live on fire?
You want to be used by God in this generation?

You have to be clean.

"Blessed are the pure in heart, for they shall see God."
(Matthew 5:8)

You don't need a seminary degree.
You don't need a big following.

You need a clean heart and a willing spirit.

And the Holy Spirit will help you get there
if you let Him do His work.

You Can't Be Full of Fire if You're Full of Filth

Too many believers want to walk in power
while still holding onto spiritual junk.

But the fire doesn't fall on clutter.
It falls on the altar of purity.

God is not looking for the most impressive.
He's looking for the most yielded.

If you're willing to say,

"Holy Spirit, come search me and clean me out,"

then the fire is not far behind.

One Thing to Remember

The Holy Spirit doesn't come to destroy you. He comes to purify you, restore you, and fill you with fire.

One Step to Take

Get alone. Get quiet.
Then say out loud:

"Holy Spirit, I invite You to search every room of my heart. Nothing is off limits. Show me what needs to go. Clean me out. I want to be pure and ready."

Be still. Listen. Respond.

One Scripture to Read Again

Titus 3:5 –

"He saved us, not because of righteous things we had done, but because of His mercy. He saved us through the washing of rebirth and renewal by the Holy Spirit."

Chapter 13: Fall in Love With Jesus Again

"Greater love has no one than this: to lay down one's life for one's friends. You are My friends if you do what I command... I have called you friends."
— John 15:13–15 (NIV)

Jesus Isn't a Concept: He's a Person

For some, Jesus is a doctrine.
For others, a symbol.
For many, a name they've heard their whole life.

But if Jesus has become anything less than real to you,
then it's no wonder your fire has faded.

You can't burn with love for an idea.
You can't have intimacy with a religion.

You were made for relationship.
Not cold, distant reverence.
But real, daily friendship with the One who laid down His life for you.

"I have called you friends," Jesus said.

He didn't save you to use you.
He saved you to know you.

And He wants you to know Him.

The Love That Laid Down Everything

Let's be clear.
Jesus didn't just talk about love.

He showed it.

He left Heaven's glory for a broken world.
He took on fragile flesh.
He was mocked, rejected, betrayed.
He was nailed to a cross not for what He had done,
but for what you and I had done.

"Greater love has no one than this: to lay down one's life for his friends."

You weren't just rescued.
You were loved.
And not because you deserved it.

"While we were still sinners, Christ died for us." (Romans 5:8)

The cross wasn't just a moment of pain.
It was a personal declaration:

"I love you. I choose you. I'll die for you."

That's not distant. That's not religious.

That's relentless love.

When Love Grows Cold

Somewhere along the way, many of us lose the wonder.

We trade intimacy for routine.
Passion for knowledge.
Closeness for performance.

We still believe in Jesus.
We still serve Him.
But we no longer burn for Him.

And Jesus, in Revelation 2, said this:

"You have forsaken your first love."

He was talking to a church that did good things,
but forgot the One who mattered most.

That could be any of us.
If we're honest, it is many of us.

We've turned relationship into religion.
Worship into performance.
Obedience into obligation.

And the fire has gone out.

The Only Way to Reignite Your Faith

It's not more sermons.
Not more Bible facts.
Not more "trying harder."

The only way to live on fire again
is to fall in love with Jesus again.

To sit with Him.
To talk to Him.
To weep in His presence.
To listen.
To worship—not for what He gives, but for who He is.

You don't need a microphone.
You don't need a spotlight.

You need a moment alone with your Savior.

How to Talk to Jesus Like a Friend

Jesus said, "I have called you friends."

So speak to Him like a friend:

Be real.

Be honest.

Say everything you've been bottling up.

Laugh with Him.

Cry in front of Him.

Sit in silence and know He's still there.

Don't perform.
Don't filter.
Just be with Him.

He's not looking for polished prayers.
He's looking for your heart.

He already knows it.
He just wants you to open it.

Reignite Your Wonder

Do you remember when you first believed?

When every worship song made you cry?
When the name "Jesus" stirred your heart?
When the cross wasn't just a message—it was a miracle?

You can feel that again.

Not because of emotion.
But because of connection.

Love grows where there's time, honesty, and presence.

You'll never fall in love with someone you only visit once a week.

Start spending unhurried time with Jesus.

He's Not Just Savior: He's Someone

Let's not forget:

Jesus is not a metaphor.

Jesus is not a philosophy.

Jesus is not a moral example.

He is a person.
Alive. Present. Listening.

He is not far off.
He is not annoyed with you.
He is not waiting for you to clean yourself up.

He is near and closer than your breath.

And He wants you back.

Not just your obedience.
Not just your knowledge.
Not just your church attendance.

You.

Love Is What Fuels the Fire

You can't sustain a fire on fear alone.
You can't walk in holiness by willpower alone.

You need love.

"We love because He first loved us." (1 John 4:19)

When you realize how deeply Jesus loves you,
you'll start loving Him back with everything.

You'll start choosing purity, not because you "have to,"
but because you don't want anything to get between you and
Him.

You'll start spending time with Him, not out of guilt,
but out of hunger.

You'll stop chasing approval, because you're already known
and loved.

That's what love does.
It rearranges your life.

Start Over Today

You don't need a fresh altar call.
You don't need another emotional high.

You need to get alone.
And simply say:

"Jesus, I want to love You again.
I miss You.
I'm tired of religion.
I want to know You again.
Help me fall in love with You."

And then talk to Him.

Fifteen minutes.
No agenda.
No script.
Just honesty.

He's Been Waiting

The most beautiful part?

You don't have to convince Jesus to come close.
He's been waiting for you.

Like the father in Luke 15,
He's scanning the horizon, arms open.

"Come back. Let's walk together again.
Let Me show you who I really am."

Don't delay.

Fall in love with Jesus again.

Not because you have to.
But because He is worth it.

One Thing to Remember

Jesus is not a system. He's not a religion. He's your Savior and your friend. He wants your heart, not just your habit.

One Step to Take

Set a timer for 15 minutes.
Find a quiet place.
No phone. No noise. No agenda.
Just sit with Jesus and talk to Him like a friend.
Tell Him everything.
Then listen.

One Scripture to Read Again

John 15:13–15 –

"Greater love has no one than this: to lay down one's life for one's friends… I have called you friends."

Chapter 14: Fuel the Fire Daily

"Because of the Lord's great love we are not consumed, for His compassions never fail. They are new every morning; great is Your faithfulness."
— Lamentations 3:22–23 (NIV)

Yesterday's Manna Won't Feed You Today

In the wilderness, God fed the Israelites with manna, fresh bread from Heaven that fell each morning.

But there was a catch:
They could only collect what they needed for that day.
If they tried to store it up for tomorrow, it would rot.

Why?

Because God wanted them to rely on Him daily.

And the same is true today.

You can't live on yesterday's time with God.
You can't carry last month's fire into today's storm.
You can't coast spiritually and expect to burn brightly.

If you want to stay on fire,
you have to feed that fire every single day.

The Danger of Coasting

Spiritual apathy rarely shows up all at once.
It creeps in when we get comfortable.

We skip prayer for a day...

We ignore the Bible because we're "too tired"...

We start to say, "I'll catch up later."

Before long, we're empty.
Cold.
Numb.

And we wonder, "Why don't I feel close to God anymore?"

The answer is simple:
Fires go out when they're not fed.

It's not about guilt.
It's about connection.

God's Love Is New Every Morning: Are You Showing Up?

Lamentations 3:23 says,

"His mercies are new every morning."

Every morning, there's a new outpouring of God's grace waiting for you.

New strength.

New peace.

New wisdom.

New joy.

But you've got to go get it.

Not because God's hiding it,
but because He wants a relationship with you.

Just like He did in the Garden with Adam,
God still walks in the cool of the day, asking,

"Where are you?"

The Secret to Staying on Fire? Daily Fuel.

It's not about hype.
It's not about emotion.
It's about habits.

Your heart follows what you do consistently.

If you eat junk every day, your body reflects it.
If you feed your mind garbage, your thoughts grow dark.

And if you starve your spirit,
don't be surprised when your passion disappears.

But here's the good news:
Just as fire fades without fuel,
it roars back to life when fed.

Make Room for God Every Day

This isn't legalism.
This is love.

You don't read the Bible to check a box.
You read it because it's God's voice.

You don't pray because you have to.
You pray because your best friend wants to talk with you.

Fires don't need fireworks.
They need kindling.

A few minutes with Jesus in the morning
can ignite something that lasts the whole day.

Start small. Stay consistent.
Show up and let Him meet you there.

The Enemy Will Fight Your Rhythm

Don't be surprised when everything tries to interrupt your
time with God.

The phone rings.

Your kids need something.

You remember a to-do list.

You "accidentally" scroll social media for 45 minutes.

It's spiritual warfare, plain and simple.

Satan doesn't care if you go to church as long as you don't spend time with Jesus the rest of the week.

Because he knows a Christian with a daily rhythm of intimacy with God is a dangerous person.

Someone who walks in peace, power, and purpose.

So guard it.
Fight for it.
Make it your non-negotiable.

How to Build a 7-Day Fire-Fueling Rhythm

You don't need to copy anyone else's quiet time.

But you do need a rhythm that works for you.

Here's a simple framework you can personalize:

Day 1 – Return to the Word

Read a chapter from the Gospels.
Ask: What is Jesus showing me about Himself today?

Day 2 – Gratitude + Praise

Write down 10 things you're thankful for.
Sing a worship song out loud.
Let your heart remember how good God is.

Day 3 – Scripture Soak

Take one short verse.
Read it slowly.
Repeat it out loud.
Ask: What does this mean for me today?

Day 4 – Listen in Prayer

Don't talk the whole time.
Sit in silence. Ask: Holy Spirit, what do You want to say?

Day 5 – Spiritual Inventory

Ask: What sin do I need to confess?
What lies am I believing?
Where do I need to obey immediately?

Day 6 – Intercede for Others

Pray for five people by name.
Ask God to move in their lives.
Let your fire serve someone else.

Day 7 – Vision + Purpose

Ask: Lord, what's my assignment this week?
How can I live on mission for You?

Don't Wait to Feel It—Start Doing It

Some people say,

"I just don't feel motivated."

But fire doesn't follow feelings.
Fire follows obedience.

When you light a match, you don't wait for it to "feel" hot.
You strike it and the flame comes.

Start small.
Stay faithful.

You'll be amazed what happens
when you show up daily to meet with God.

What Happens When You Feed the Fire

When you fuel the fire daily:

Your mind becomes clearer.

Your heart becomes softer.

Your words become more powerful.

Your life begins to reflect Jesus not just on Sunday, but every day.

This is what Jesus meant when He said:

"Remain in Me, and I will remain in you." (John 15:4)

You don't visit Him once a week.
You remain and your life starts to bear fruit.

One Thing to Remember

You can't burn for God if you're living off yesterday's flame.
The fire is daily—and so is the invitation.

One Step to Take

Build a 7-day Bible and prayer rhythm that you actually look forward to.
Start with just 15 minutes a day.
Choose a place. Set a time. Stick with it.

Let it become your new normal.

One Scripture to Read Again

Lamentations 3:22–23 –

"Because of the Lord's great love we are not consumed, for His compassions never fail.
They are new every morning; great is Your faithfulness."

Chapter 15: Spiritual Warfare Is Real—and You're in It

"For we wrestle not against flesh and blood, but against principalities, against powers, against the rulers of the darkness of this world, against spiritual wickedness in high places."
— Ephesians 6:12 (KJV)

You're Not Just Struggling: You're at War

It's not just stress.
It's not just fatigue.
It's not just bad luck.

What you're feeling?
What you're facing?
It's a battle.

There is a real enemy.
There is a real war.
And you are not exempt.

If you belong to Jesus, you've been drafted.

Not into a playground.
Into a battlefield.

And whether you realize it or not, you're already in it.

The Devil Doesn't Want to Scare You: He Wants to Numb You

You might expect Satan to show up with red horns and fire.
But most of the time, he doesn't need to scare you.
He just needs to distract you.

Numb you with comfort.

Fill your schedule with busyness.

Entangle you in addiction.

Whisper lies that sound close to the truth.

"Even Satan disguises himself as an angel of light." (2 Corinthians 11:14)

The greatest trick of the enemy is making you think there is no battle.
That life is just "hard."
That you're just "tired."
That it's just "your personality."

No.
It's war.

And if you don't fight back,
you'll become a casualty without even realizing it.

Wake Up to What's Really Happening

Ephesians 6:12 pulls back the curtain:

"We wrestle not against flesh and blood..."

Your fight isn't against your spouse.
Your fight isn't against your boss.
Your fight isn't against your depression, anxiety, or past.

Your fight is spiritual.

There are forces of darkness trying to steal your peace.

There are demonic assignments designed to derail your purpose.

There are temptations crafted to numb your passion and crush your faith.

And you don't beat this kind of warfare with willpower.
You beat it with weapons from Heaven.

The Armor of God Is Not Optional

God didn't leave you defenseless.

He gave you armor.
He gave you a sword.
He gave you authority.

But if you leave your armor in the closet,
don't be surprised when the enemy lands a hit.

"Put on the full armor of God..." (Ephesians 6:11)

Let's break it down:

1. The Belt of Truth

Wrap yourself in God's Word.
When lies come, truth holds everything together.

2. The Breastplate of Righteousness

Live clean. Stay right with God.
Don't give Satan a foothold.

3. The Shoes of Peace

Be anchored in the Gospel.
Stand firm no matter what chaos hits.

4. The Shield of Faith

Use your faith to deflect doubt, fear, and temptation.

5. The Helmet of Salvation

Guard your thoughts. Remember whose you are.

6. The Sword of the Spirit

The Word of God—spoken out loud—is your weapon.

You're Not Fighting for Victory—You're Fighting From It

Jesus already crushed the enemy.

"Having disarmed the powers and authorities, He made a public spectacle of them, triumphing over them by the cross." (Colossians 2:15)

You're not trying to win a war.
You're enforcing a victory.

But to do that, you have to fight.

Not in your own strength.

Not with anger or fear.

But with Scripture, prayer, and worship.

Recognize the Devil's Favorite Strategies

Here's how the enemy attacks most believers:

1. Distraction

He'll do anything to keep you out of God's presence.

2. Deception

He twists the truth just enough to make it believable.

3. Accusation

He brings up your past to make you doubt your identity.

4. Division

He separates you from community so you're easier to pick off.

5. Delay

He convinces you there's always "tomorrow" to get serious with God.

But you can call his bluff.
You have the name of Jesus.
You have the Word of God.
You have the Holy Spirit inside of you.

You're not a victim.
You're a warrior.

Speak Scripture Because the Devil Hates Truth

When Jesus was tempted in the wilderness,
He didn't argue.
He didn't explain.
He didn't whine.

He quoted Scripture.

"It is written…" (Matthew 4:4)

That's your sword.
It's time to start swinging it.

Pick a verse. Memorize it.
When the lies come speak truth out loud.

Here's a few to start with:

"Greater is He that is in me than he that is in the world." (1 John 4:4)

"No weapon formed against me shall prosper." (Isaiah 54:17)

"Resist the devil, and he will flee from you." (James 4:7)

"God has not given me a spirit of fear, but of power, love, and a sound mind." (2 Timothy 1:7)

You Are a Threat When You Live Awake

The devil doesn't fear a lukewarm Christian.

He fears a surrendered, scripture-soaked, Spirit-filled believer who knows they're at war and walks in the authority of Heaven.

You don't have to be perfect.
You just have to be aware.

Fight from your knees.

Fight with your praise.

Fight with your mouth full of the Word of God.

This is real.
And the more on fire you become,
the more you'll feel the heat of the battle.

But don't be afraid.

Because the fire in you is stronger than the fire around you.

One Thing to Remember

Spiritual warfare is not symbolic. It's real. But so is your victory in Christ. Suit up. Speak the Word. Stand your ground.

One Step to Take

Choose one Scripture from this chapter that speaks to your current battle.
Memorize it.
Say it out loud every morning this week.
When the enemy whispers, shout it back.

One Scripture to Read Again

Ephesians 6:12 –

"For we wrestle not against flesh and blood, but against principalities, against powers, against the rulers of the darkness of this world, against spiritual wickedness in high places."

Chapter 16: Worship Like Heaven Is Watching

"About midnight Paul and Silas were praying and singing hymns to God, and the other prisoners were listening to them. Suddenly there was such a violent earthquake that the foundations of the prison were shaken."
—Acts 16:25–26

The Power of a Midnight Song

Let's begin with a question: If we were thrown into prison for sharing the gospel, stripped, beaten, and chained in the deepest, darkest cell—what would we do?

Most of us would be begging God to get us out. Some of us might fall silent, lost in fear or confusion. But Paul and Silas? They sang.

They weren't singing because they were comfortable. They weren't worshiping because it "felt good." They worshiped because they knew who God was, even when the world around them looked like chaos.

And Heaven answered.

The ground trembled. Chains shattered. Doors flew open. God didn't just show up. He shook the place.

This wasn't just about deliverance from prison. It was a revelation: Worship is not passive. Worship is power.

Worship Is a Weapon

We've watered worship down. We've made it about style, volume, and song preference.

But worship isn't about personal taste.
Worship is spiritual warfare.

When you sing to God in the middle of pain, you push back darkness. When you raise your hands in surrender, you defy the enemy. When you praise Him in the middle of a storm, you declare, "My God still reigns."

That's what Paul and Silas did. And that's why the prison couldn't hold them.

Worship is the war cry of the surrendered soul.

Why Heaven Moves When You Worship

God isn't insecure. He doesn't need our songs to feel good about Himself.

So why does worship matter?

Because worship is about alignment. When you worship, you acknowledge that He is God, and you are not. You dethrone self. You silence fear. You exalt the One who deserves it all.

Scripture says God inhabits the praises of His people (Psalm 22:3). That means He doesn't just listen. He moves in.

The world changes when God shows up.

Worship Can Set Others Free

Don't miss what Acts 16 really says. It wasn't just Paul and Silas who were set free. The Bible says, "everyone's chains came loose."

Their worship didn't just unlock their own breakthrough. It created an atmosphere for freedom for everyone.

What if your worship isn't just about you?

What if your worship is what helps your spouse find hope again?

What if your song is what gives your kids strength when they're afraid?

What if your praise at church opens the door for someone next to you to encounter God for the first time?

Worship is contagious. It sets a tone. It breaks spiritual ceilings.

Your Voice Matters More Than You Think

Some people hold back in worship because they think, "I can't sing." Or, "It's not my personality." Or, "I'm too broken."

But here's the truth: Heaven isn't listening for perfect pitch. It's listening for pure hearts.

Worship doesn't have to sound beautiful. It just has to be real.

David danced before the Lord in his undergarments. Mary broke a jar of perfume and wiped Jesus' feet with her hair. The leper fell to the ground in gratitude. These weren't rehearsed performances. They were messy, honest, passionate expressions of love.

Don't worry about how it looks or sounds. Just make sure it's coming from your heart.

When You Don't Feel Like Worshiping

Let's be honest. Sometimes you don't feel like praising. You feel tired, numb, distracted. That's exactly when you need to worship the most.

In those moments, praise becomes a sacrifice. And that sacrifice is precious to God.

Hebrews 13:15 says, "Through Jesus, therefore, let us continually offer to God a sacrifice of praise."

Sacrifices aren't easy. They cost you something. They stretch you. But they move the heart of God.

If you wait until you feel like it, you'll rarely do it. Worship is a choice before it's a feeling.

Worship Isn't Just for Sundays

If your only worship time is at church, you're starving your spirit.

Think about it. If you only ate once a week, how long would you survive?

Worship needs to become part of your daily rhythm. Not because God is keeping score, but because your soul was designed to glorify Him. When you starve your worship, your fire starts to fade.

Start simple:

One song during your commute.

A five-minute playlist while you journal.

Singing a short chorus before reading Scripture.

It doesn't have to be long or loud. It just needs to be real.

Worship Builds an Altar of Fire

In the Old Testament, altars were where sacrifices were offered and where fire fell from Heaven.

You don't need a stone altar anymore. You are the altar.

Romans 12:1 tells us to present our bodies as a living sacrifice, holy and pleasing to God. That's worship.

Every time you say, "God, You're worthy, even when I don't understand," you place yourself on that altar again. And when you stay on the altar, the fire keeps burning.

Heaven Is Watching and Listening

Jesus said in John 4:23 that the Father is seeking true worshipers, those who worship in spirit and in truth.

Heaven isn't looking for polished performances.
It's searching for hearts that burn.

So what happens when Heaven finds someone like that?

Chains break.

Strongholds fall.

Healing begins.

Revival ignites.

Worship invites the supernatural into the natural. And when you do it with all your heart, angels take notice. Demons tremble. God draws near.

Make Worship a Daily Fire-Starter

Here's a challenge: For the next seven days, start your morning with worship before anything else. Before you check your phone. Before you read the news. Before coffee.

Play one song.
Lift your voice.
Invite His presence.

Watch what happens to your mood, your thoughts, your reactions, your peace.

You weren't made to live lukewarm. You were made to live in awe.

One Thing to Remember

Worship isn't a warm-up. It's a weapon that shifts the atmosphere, breaks spiritual chains, and draws Heaven to earth.

One Step to Take

Start each day this week with worship. Choose one song that stirs your heart. Sing it, pray it, and journal what God shows you.

Example playlist:

"Gratitude" – Brandon Lake

"The Blessing" – Kari Jobe & Cody Carnes

"Worthy of It All" – CeCe Winans

"Come Rest on Us" – Maverick City Music

"Defender" – Upper Room

"King of Kings" – Hillsong Worship

"Battle Belongs" – Phil Wickham

One Scripture to Read Again

Acts 16:25–26
"About midnight Paul and Silas were praying and singing hymns to God, and the other prisoners were listening to them. Suddenly there was such a violent earthquake that the foundations of the prison were shaken. At once all the prison doors flew open, and everyone's chains came loose."

Chapter 17: Fast Until You're Free

"Is not this the kind of fasting I have chosen: to loose the chains of injustice and untie the cords of the yoke, to set the oppressed free and break every yoke?"
—Isaiah 58:6

Fasting: The Forgotten Weapon

In today's world, fasting has been hijacked by wellness gurus and diet plans. You'll hear it called "intermittent fasting" or "cleansing", but what most people are doing has nothing to do with the kind of fasting God calls us to.

Fasting in the Bible isn't about self-improvement. It's about spiritual breakthrough.

It's about seeking God with such desperation that you're willing to lay down even your most basic need—food—to say, "God, I want You more."

Fasting is not a hunger strike. It's an invitation to fire.

Why Fast? Because Some Chains Only Break This Way

In Mark 9, a father brought his demon-tormented son to Jesus' disciples, but they couldn't drive the demon out. Later, Jesus said, "This kind can come out only by prayer and fasting." (Mark 9:29)

Did you catch that?

There are some strongholds, some stubborn sins, some generational curses, some emotional bondages that will only break through fasting.

Fasting is spiritual dynamite. It weakens the flesh. It humbles the heart. And it releases power from Heaven.

Fasting Isn't Punishment: It's Preparation

When Jesus began His public ministry, He didn't start with a miracle. He didn't jump into preaching. He fasted.

Forty days. Alone. In the wilderness.

Why?

Because fasting sharpens spiritual sight. It silences distractions. It prepares the soul to be a vessel of power.

Before God uses you greatly, He often empties you deeply.

Fasting is a way to say, "Lord, empty me of everything that's not from You so You can fill me with all that is."

What Breaks When You Fast?

Isaiah 58:6 is one of the clearest and most powerful passages on fasting in Scripture. God says:

"Is not this the kind of fasting I have chosen:
to loose the chains of injustice
and untie the cords of the yoke,
to set the oppressed free
and break every yoke?"

That means when you fast:

Chains are loosened

Heavy yokes are broken

Hidden sin is exposed

Pride is crushed

Healing begins

Your spirit comes alive

Fasting is God's way of breaking through spiritual numbness and setting fire to a cold heart.

It's Not About the Food

If you fast but don't pray, if you go hungry but don't draw near to God, you've just skipped a meal.

Fasting without prayer is dieting.

The goal isn't just to stop eating. The goal is to press into God's presence, to repent deeply, to listen closely, and to let the Holy Spirit move freely in your life.

Jesus said, "When you fast..." (Matthew 6:16), not "If." Fasting isn't for spiritual elites. It's for anyone who's serious about God.

What Happens During a Fast

Let's be honest. Fasting isn't glamorous. Sometimes you get headaches. Sometimes you feel weak. Sometimes your flesh throws a tantrum.

But in those moments, your spirit begins to rise. The noise of the world fades. Your cravings lose their grip. Your ears start tuning into Heaven.

As your stomach empties, your soul fills.

When you fast with humility and purpose, God meets you in ways food never could.

How to Fast: Start Where You Are

You don't need to go 40 days without food. You don't need to lock yourself in a cave.

Start small. Start real.

Here are some ideas:

Fast one meal today and spend that time in prayer.

Fast from sunup to sundown and read Isaiah 58 during lunch.

Fast from social media for 24 hours and use that time to journal and worship.

Fast one day this week and pray specifically for breakthrough in an area where you've been stuck.

Ask the Holy Spirit what kind of fast He's calling you to—and obey.

When You Fast, Don't Show Off: Press In

Jesus warned us not to fast to impress people. In Matthew 6:17–18, He says:

"But when you fast, anoint your head and wash your face, so that it will not be obvious to others that you are fasting, but only to your Father… and your Father, who sees what is done in secret, will reward you."

Fasting isn't about being seen. It's about being set apart.

It's a secret weapon with public results.

Testimonies of Fasting Fire

Throughout history, fasting has marked every revival:

Ezra fasted for protection before a dangerous journey.

Esther called a three-day fast to turn a nation's fate.

Daniel fasted and received visions from God.

Jesus fasted before defeating the devil in the wilderness.

The early church fasted before appointing leaders and sending missionaries.

If you want to see God move like He did in Scripture, you need to live like they did in Scripture.

And that includes fasting.

Fasting Changes YOU First

Here's the truth: Sometimes, you fast expecting the situation to change, and God uses it to change you first.

That hidden sin?
That prideful attitude?
That fear you've been carrying?
Fasting surfaces it all.

It's not always comfortable, but it's always worth it.

Freedom Costs Something

We want freedom. But we want it cheap.

Fasting reminds us that freedom often comes at the price of self-denial. That's the way of the cross. That's the path of power.

If you want to be on fire, you've got to empty yourself of what dims your flame.

Your Turn to Fast and Be Free

Don't just read this chapter and move on. Step into the fire. Fast.

Pick a day. Skip a meal. Go before God with an open Bible and a surrendered heart.

Say, "Lord, I want You more than I want food. I want breakthrough more than I want comfort. I want freedom more than I want ease."

And then watch what He does.

One Thing to Remember

Fasting is not about starvation. It's about surrender. It's a divine invitation to break chains, gain clarity, and ignite your soul with God's power.

One Step to Take

Choose one meal or one full day this week to fast and pray. During that time, read Isaiah 58 and journal any conviction, direction, or insight the Lord gives you.

One Scripture to Read Again

Isaiah 58:6 -
"Is not this the kind of fasting I have chosen: to loose the chains of injustice and untie the cords of the yoke, to set the oppressed free and break every yoke?"

Chapter 18: You're an Ambassador, Not a Spectator

"We are therefore Christ's ambassadors, as though God were making his appeal through us."
—2 Corinthians 5:20

Watching Isn't the Same as Witnessing

It's easy to watch others live bold lives for Christ and think, "That's for them, not for me."
You admire missionaries. You're moved by street preachers. You repost Christian quotes. Maybe you even attend a church where people are fired up about Jesus.

But here's the truth:

God didn't save you to sit in the bleachers. He called you to the battlefield.

You weren't rescued from sin to become a religious spectator.
You were redeemed for a purpose to represent the King of Kings.

That's what it means to be an ambassador of Christ.

The Job Description of an Ambassador

In the natural world, an ambassador is a high-ranking representative sent from one nation to another. They speak with authority, represent the interests of their leader, and carry the weight of their kingdom's message.

Now read 2 Corinthians 5:20 again:

"We are therefore Christ's ambassadors, as though God were making His appeal through us."

God is not using angels to share the gospel.
He's using you.
You're His mouthpiece.
His hands.
His messenger.

You don't need a seminary degree to qualify. You don't need a pulpit. You don't need to have it all figured out.

You just need to be available.

The Crowd Can't Change the World: But a Witness Can

Imagine a courtroom full of spectators. The judge doesn't ask for their opinion. The outcome of the case doesn't depend on what the crowd believes or feels.

The verdict often hinges on the witness.

Why?

Because the witness has seen something.
The witness knows something.
The witness stands and tells the truth.

In Acts 1:8, Jesus didn't say, "You will be my spectators."

He said, "You will be my witnesses."

You're Already Qualified

Think you don't have what it takes to be used by God?

Let's take a look at a few of the "ambassadors" Jesus personally selected:

A fisherman with a hot temper (Peter)

A corrupt tax collector (Matthew)

A woman with five ex-husbands and a bad reputation (John 4)

A religious terrorist (Paul)

What do they all have in common?

They encountered Jesus.
And when they did, they couldn't keep it to themselves.

You don't need perfection.
You need passion.
You need the fire of the Holy Spirit and the willingness to open your mouth.

Your Testimony Has Power

Revelation 12:11 says,
"They triumphed over [Satan] by the blood of the Lamb and by the word of their testimony..."

Your story of what Jesus has done in your life is spiritual ammunition.

When you share what God has rescued you from...
When you talk about how He forgave you...
When you speak of the peace He gave you in the storm...

You are wielding a weapon against hell.

Someone needs to hear your story. Someone's breakthrough is on the other side of your obedience.

From Silence to Sent

Too many believers are spiritually silent.

We go to church.
We say grace before meals.
We might even wear a cross necklace.

But when was the last time you actually told someone about Jesus?

Paul said,

"Woe to me if I do not preach the gospel!" (1 Corinthians 9:16)

This wasn't just for full-time preachers. It's for anyone who has been changed by the cross.

Jesus didn't ask us to make converts. He commanded us to make disciples.
And disciples don't stay silent.

Spectators Stay Comfortable. Ambassadors Change History.

The early church was full of fire, not fans. They didn't just sing songs—they risked their lives.

They didn't blend in. They stood out.
They didn't wait for someone else. They said, "Here I am. Send me."

Look around today.

The world doesn't need more "nice Christians."
It needs bold ambassadors.
People who know who they represent.
People who speak truth with love.
People who aren't ashamed of the gospel even if it costs them.

Don't Let Fear Muzzle Your Mission

What's stopping you?

Fear of rejection?

Worry about what people will think?

Feeling like you don't know enough?

Let me tell you something: the Holy Spirit will give you the words.

You don't need a perfect presentation. You just need a willing heart.

Jesus said,
"Whoever acknowledges me before others, I will also acknowledge before my Father in heaven." (Matthew 10:32)

But He also warned,
"Whoever disowns me before others, I will disown before my Father in heaven." (v. 33)

You don't want to meet Jesus someday and realize you stayed quiet out of fear.

What If You're the Only Jesus They Ever See?

That coworker.
That classmate.
That friend at the gym.
That cousin who's drifting.

You might be their only window to the gospel.

Don't waste it.

People are searching for hope. They're numbing their pain with screens, success, and substances. They're looking for something real.

And you carry the most real, most powerful, most eternity-changing truth the world has ever known.

Tell it.

Share Your Testimony This Week

Don't wait for the perfect moment.
Create one.

Send a voice memo to a friend about what God's done in your life.

Text your story to a sibling who's far from God.

Sit with your child and tell them how Jesus saved you.

Post a video online sharing your "before and after" story.

You don't need a platform. You have a pulse.

That means your mission isn't over.

One Thing to Remember

You weren't saved to spectate. You were called to represent the King. Heaven is counting on you to share what you've seen, heard, and experienced.

One Step to Take

This week, share your testimony with one person. Don't overthink it. Just tell them what Jesus has done in your life.

One Scripture to Read Again

2 Corinthians 5:20
"We are therefore Christ's ambassadors, as though God were making his appeal through us. We implore you on Christ's behalf: Be reconciled to God."

Chapter 19: Build an Altar, Not a Platform

"But when you pray, go into your room, close the door and pray to your Father, who is unseen. Then your Father, who sees what is done in secret, will reward you."
—Matthew 6:6

The Fire That Falls in Secret

In today's world, platforms are everywhere.

Social media platforms. Personal brands. Ministries with logos and slogans. Sermons livestreamed, devotionals posted, hashtags trending.

But long before God ever uses a man or woman publicly, He forms them privately.

The most powerful fire doesn't fall on a platform. It falls on the altar—and altars are built in secret.

In Matthew 6:6, Jesus gives one of the clearest commands about prayer:

Go into your room. Close the door.
Talk to the Father no one else sees.
And the reward will come—not in likes or applause—but in divine intimacy.

Let that settle in:

He sees what's done in secret.
Not what's posted. Not what's praised. Not what's popular.

God Is Not Looking for Celebrities: He's Looking for Surrender

The Bible is full of people who were formed in hidden places:

Moses was called at a burning bush in the wilderness.

David was anointed king while still tending sheep.

Jesus spent 30 years in obscurity before 3 years of public ministry.

Paul spent time in the desert being shaped by God before he ever preached to crowds.

We live in a world where everyone wants to be seen, followed, and known.
But God's question is:
Do you still come to Me when no one's watching?

The Altar Is Where You Die and He Lives

In the Old Testament, altars were places of sacrifice.

Blood was spilled. Flesh was burned. Offerings were laid down.

And today, though the physical altar may not be made of stone, the invitation is still the same:

Bring yourself. Lay down your pride. Burn up your backup plans. Offer your obedience.

Romans 12:1 says,

"Offer your bodies as a living sacrifice, holy and pleasing to God—this is your true and proper worship."

True fire falls where something is willing to die.

If you want to stay on fire, you must keep building an altar, day after day, moment by moment.

The Secret Place Is Where the Fire Stays Lit

Let's be honest.

Most people don't fall away from God because of one major sin.
They drift because they neglect the secret place.

They forget to pray.
They stop opening the Word.
They replace intimacy with activity.
They get busy doing for God and forget to just be with God.

If you want to stay spiritually sharp, you must prioritize time alone with Jesus, not because it checks a box, but because it keeps your heart burning.

In Luke 5:16, we read:

"Jesus often withdrew to lonely places and prayed."

If Jesus, the Son of God, needed secret time with the Father... how much more do we?

Your Soul Is Starving for the Secret Place

Think about it.

How many times have you scrolled through your phone for 30 minutes...
...only to feel tired, anxious, or numb afterward?

Now compare that to 30 minutes in God's presence.

You walk out with peace.
You're reminded of truth.
You stop carrying things God never meant for you to bear.

The secret place is soul food.
It's oxygen for your spirit.
It's where you're reminded who you are, who God is, and why it matters.

There's Power in Hiddenness

When you build a platform, you're tempted to perform.
When you build an altar, you're trained to surrender.

When you chase attention, you'll burn out.
When you chase Jesus, you'll burn bright.

The devil doesn't mind if you're religious in public as long as you're weak in private.

He doesn't mind if you go to church, serve, post verses, and wear the T-shirt, as long as you never touch the power of the secret place.

But when you start praying behind closed doors…
When you weep over your sin in private…
When you hunger for His presence more than man's praise…

That's when you become dangerous.

Are You Building with Straw or Stone?

In 1 Corinthians 3:13, Paul warns:

"…their work will be shown for what it is, because the Day will bring it to light. It will be revealed with fire…"

There's a fire coming.

Every ministry. Every message. Every motive.
It will all be tested.

The question is: Will it survive the flame?

If you're building for yourself—your name, your fame—it's straw.
But if you're building for Jesus on your knees, with humility, in love, then it's stone.

Build with stone.
Build with truth.
Build with fire-proof devotion.

Your Public Life Is Only as Strong as Your Private One

Character is formed when no one's clapping.
Anointing is cultivated when no one's watching.
Fire is fed when no one's looking.

Let me ask you:

Do you crave time with God more than time with people?

Do you love Jesus when the lights are off and the crowd is gone?

Would you still follow Him if no one ever noticed?

If not... it's time to rebuild the altar.

How to Build an Altar in Your Life

You don't need a stage.
You need a chair. A Bible. A moment.

Here's how you can start:

Pick a time. Early in the morning, during lunch, or before bed. Make it consistent.

Pick a place. A closet, a corner, a car seat. Somewhere without distraction.

Pick a posture. Kneel. Sit. Lay flat. Worship. Cry. Just be real.

Open the Word. Let God speak before you do.

Pray raw prayers. Don't perform. Pour out your soul.

Stay until it burns. Don't rush it. Stay until your heart catches fire again.

This is how revival starts in you.

God Rewards What's Done in Secret

You may never be known by man.
You may never get invited to speak or post viral videos.
But if your life is hidden in Christ…
If your altar is built in love…

He sees. And He will reward.

One Thing to Remember

God doesn't need your platform. He desires your altar.
What's done in secret has eternal impact.

One Step to Take

Spend at least 15 minutes today alone with God. No music, no
phone, no Bible study plan. Just you and Him.

One Scripture to Read Again

Matthew 6:6
"But when you pray, go into your room, close the door and
pray to your Father, who is unseen. Then your Father, who
sees what is done in secret, will reward you."

Chapter 20: Get Around People Who Burn

"As iron sharpens iron, so one person sharpens another."
—Proverbs 27:17

You Were Never Meant to Burn Alone

Picture a roaring fire. Logs stacked together, blazing hot. The flame dances, heat radiates, and light fills the space.

Now picture one log pulled from that fire and placed off to the side.
What happens?

It cools.
The flame dims.
The light fades.
Eventually, it goes out.

That's what happens to Christians who try to walk alone.

You might burn for a little while, but without the heat of community, without the sharpening of others, your fire will slowly die.

The enemy knows this. He wants you isolated. Independent. Proud. Offended.
Because a lone believer is a vulnerable believer.

But a believer surrounded by others who burn for Jesus?
That's unstoppable.

Fire Is Contagious

You know this already.

Spend time around gossips: you'll start to gossip.

Hang out with complainers: you'll become negative.

Sit with lukewarm Christians: you'll feel justified staying stagnant.

But get around people who are on fire for God, people who are hungry for His Word, eager to pray, bold in their faith, and you'll catch flame.

You'll be convicted.
You'll be inspired.
You'll be sharpened.

Just like Proverbs 27:17 says:
"As iron sharpens iron, so one person sharpens another."

We weren't designed to sharpen ourselves. We need other believers.
Not perfect ones. Just real ones. People who love Jesus and want more of Him.

Even Jesus Didn't Go It Alone

When God came to Earth in the flesh, He didn't isolate Himself.

Jesus walked with a community.

He had twelve disciples that He taught, ate with, prayed with, and poured into.
He shared in their weakness. He corrected them. He loved them.

And even within the twelve, He had a closer circle of three: Peter, James, and John.

If Jesus needed people around Him… who are we to think we don't?

Christianity is not a solo sport. It's a team battle.

You were saved into a body. You were never meant to be the whole thing on your own.

Godly Community Keeps You Aligned

Think of community like spiritual accountability.

When you drift, they call you back.
When you're dry, they pray over you.
When you sin, they help restore you gently (Galatians 6:1).
When you're discouraged, they lift your head.
When you feel weak, they remind you who you are.

A real godly friend doesn't just pat you on the back. They point you to Jesus.

Sometimes, they'll offend your comfort zone to awaken your calling.
Sometimes, they'll ask you hard questions to keep you from hiding.
Sometimes, they'll see something in you that you've forgotten.

That's the kind of sharpening Proverbs 27:17 is talking about.

Not shallow "Sunday smiles," but deep relationships that challenge, stretch, and grow you.

The Early Church Burned Together

Go back to the Book of Acts.
After Pentecost, the fire fell, and what happened?

"They devoted themselves to the apostles' teaching and to fellowship, to the breaking of bread and to prayer." —Acts 2:42

They lived in community.
They shared meals.

They prayed together.
They worshiped together.
They grew together.

And it didn't stop there. They also evangelized together.

That kind of unity wasn't optional. It was essential.
It was the fuel that kept the fire alive.

You want to stay on fire for Jesus?
Don't just go to church. Be the Church. Live like the Church.

Warning: Not All "Community" Keeps You Burning

Let's pause for a moment.

Community is powerful. But it's also dangerous if it's the wrong kind.

Some people will put out your fire faster than any temptation ever could.

Watch out for those who:

Mock conviction and celebrate compromise

Downplay sin and twist Scripture

Constantly stir up division or drama

Love the world more than the Word

Keep you "comfortable" in your lukewarmness

Paul warned about this:

"Do not be misled: 'Bad company corrupts good character.'"
—1 Corinthians 15:33

So yes, get around people. But make sure they're people who burn.

How to Find or Build a Community That Ignites Your Faith

If you're reading this and thinking, "But I don't have anyone like that in my life," you're not alone.

Many believers feel isolated.
Some are the only Christians in their family.
Others are surrounded by half-hearted religion but no burning passion.

So what do you do?

1. Start with Prayer

Ask God to bring people into your life who will sharpen and strengthen you.

He knows who you need.

2. Take a Risk

Join a small group. Go to a Bible study. Say hello to someone at church.

Most community starts with awkwardness but ends in intimacy.

3. Be What You're Looking For

Want bold friends? Be bold.
Want praying friends? Start praying for others.
Want honest friends? Be honest first.

You'll attract what you practice.

4. Start Something If Nothing Exists

You don't need permission to gather in Jesus' name.

Invite two or three people over for coffee and Scripture.
Start a Zoom call to pray weekly.
Form a group text for daily encouragement.

Wherever two or three are gathered, Jesus promised He'd be there.

Community Doesn't Replace Intimacy: It Protects It

Let's be clear: people can't take the place of Jesus.
But they can point you back to Him when you wander.

They can remind you of your identity when you forget.
They can call you out when you're drifting.
They can walk beside you when the road gets hard.

Your private time with God is the flame.
Your community is the woodpile that keeps it going.

Together, you can burn brighter, longer, and stronger.

Don't Let Isolation Extinguish What God Started

The truth is: many people fall away alone.

No one knew they were struggling.

No one asked the hard questions.

No one saw them slipping until they were gone.

Let that not be you.

Get around people who burn.
People who challenge your faith, not coddle your comfort.
People who love you enough to correct you.
People who push you closer to the cross.

You may not need a crowd.
But you absolutely need a few on-fire believers to walk with.

One Thing to Remember

You will either be sharpened by the fire of others or slowly grow cold alone. Choose wisely who surrounds you.

One Step to Take

Text or call one believer today and ask to meet up, pray together, or start a group. Don't wait for community. Create it.

One Scripture to Read Again

Proverbs 27:17
"As iron sharpens iron, so one person sharpens another."

Chapter 21: Guard What God Has Given You

"Timothy, guard what has been entrusted to your care. Turn away from godless chatter and the opposing ideas of what is falsely called knowledge."
—1 Timothy 6:20

What God Puts In, the Enemy Tries to Steal

Every time God deposits something in your spirit—a word, a conviction, a calling—the enemy starts plotting how to take it.

It's not always obvious. Sometimes it's not a frontal assault but a subtle erosion.

Satan is a thief.
He doesn't knock at the front door with horns and a pitchfork. He slips in through distractions. He steals joy with anxiety. He whispers half-truths until we question the whole truth.

Jesus warned us plainly:

"When anyone hears the message about the kingdom and does not understand it, the evil one comes and snatches away what was sown in their heart."
(Matthew 13:19)

I remember the first time I truly surrendered to Christ. I was on fire. I couldn't stop reading Scripture. Worship moved me to tears. I shared my faith with boldness.

But a few weeks in, things started shifting.

I got busier. The prayers got shorter. My heart started cooling. I didn't even realize it until one day I opened my Bible and felt... nothing.

The same fire that once burned hot was flickering.

It wasn't because I stopped believing.

It was because I stopped guarding.

The Subtle Drift Is the Real Danger

Most people don't renounce their faith in a moment.

They just drift.

One skipped devotional becomes two. One compromise becomes a habit. One toxic voice becomes louder than God's.

And it all feels so reasonable.

You say,
"God understands I'm tired."
"God knows my heart."
"This isn't really hurting anyone."

But little by little, the flame dies down not because someone blew it out, but because we stopped feeding it.

Think of a fire.
You don't need to pour water on it to kill it.
Just stop adding wood.

"The fire on the altar must be kept burning; it must not go out."
(Leviticus 6:12)

The same is true for the fire inside you.

What's Stealing Your Fire?

Do a spiritual inventory.

What's got your attention more than Jesus lately?

What do you run to for peace when life gets hard: God or something else?

Who in your life leaves you feeling further from God after you spend time with them?

God isn't asking to shame you. He's trying to protect you.

The enemy is cunning. He'll offer you a counterfeit fire that burns fast but leaves you empty: entertainment, comfort, attention, distractions.

But only God's fire purifies, empowers, and endures.

Revival Dies Without Watchmen

The Great Welsh Revival of 1904 saw over 100,000 people come to Christ in a single year. Churches were packed. Bars shut down. Crime dropped to near zero. It was a move of God no one could deny.

But within a few short years, it faded.

Why?

Because it wasn't guarded.

People didn't disciple the new believers. They didn't root the revival in the Word. Emotional fire wasn't anchored by spiritual discipline.

What God starts, we're called to sustain through obedience, community, and spiritual vigilance.

You are the keeper of the flame in your life.
If you don't guard it, you'll lose it.

Guarding Takes Effort, But So Does Regret

Paul didn't tell Timothy to light the fire. God had already done that.

He told him to guard it.

"Fan into flame the gift of God…"
(2 Timothy 1:6)

That takes effort.

Effort in your schedule.
Effort in your relationships.
Effort in your thoughts.

Spiritual laziness leads to spiritual loss. No one grows close to Jesus by accident.

Guarding is Worship

Think boundaries are legalistic?

Read Romans 12:1:

"Offer your bodies as a living sacrifice, holy and pleasing to God—this is your true and proper worship."

Turning off a show that glorifies darkness is worship.
Walking away from gossip is worship.
Saying no to that text or that party is worship.

It says, "God, You are worth more than this compromise."

Culture is Loud, but Holiness is Louder in Heaven

Culture doesn't want you to guard your heart.

It wants access.

Access to your attention, your values, your identity.

But holiness will always look strange to a culture that celebrates sin. It did in the Bible. It does now.

Noah was mocked.
Daniel was targeted.
Paul was imprisoned.
Jesus was crucified.

But they didn't lose their fire.
They guarded it and the world was changed because of it.

Guard Your Mind: That's Where the War Starts

The mind is the battlefield. Every lie you believe starts there. Every compromise you justify takes root there.

That's why Scripture says:

"Take every thought captive to obey Christ."
(2 Corinthians 10:5)

If you let impure, prideful, or fearful thoughts camp in your mind, they will build a fortress in your heart.

You can't think holy and live defeated.
You can't think defeated and live holy.
Guard your mind.

Guard Your Time: Your Calendar Preaches

Look at your calendar. It tells the story of your priorities.

Are you scheduling time with God or fitting Him in when there's a gap?

Jesus was the Son of God, but He withdrew often to be alone with the Father (Luke 5:16). If He needed solitude, how much more do we?

The world is loud. Social media is addictive. Entertainment is endless.

But the secret place still changes lives.

Guard Your Relationships: Fire Needs the Right Fuel

Some friends fuel your flame.
Others pour water on it.

It doesn't mean you cut people off, but you do need to be wise about who you walk closely with.

"Walk with the wise and become wise, for a companion of fools suffers harm."
(Proverbs 13:20)

Jesus spent time with sinners, but He didn't let them set His standard. His closest friends were people who walked in the same direction.

Surround yourself with people who remind you who you are, not who you used to be.

Guarding Isn't Fear: It's Focus

This isn't about being scared of sin.

It's about being serious about your calling.

It's about loving Jesus so much that you won't let anything get in the way.

It's about finishing well.

You've been entrusted with something eternal: your testimony, your influence, your fire.

Don't let anyone or anything steal that.

When the enemy whispers, "You're being too intense,"
Remember:
Noah built the ark in the sun.
Daniel prayed through the threat.

Paul preached in chains.
Jesus bled for you.

You're not crazy for being careful. You're wise for being watchful.

One Thing to Remember

The fire God placed in you is sacred. Guard it with everything you've got because it's worth everything.

One Step to Take

Write down the top 3 distractions pulling you away from God, and draw one clear boundary to protect your time, mind, or heart this week.

One Scripture to Read Again

1 Timothy 6:20
"Timothy, guard what has been entrusted to your care. Turn away from godless chatter and the opposing ideas of what is falsely called knowledge."

Chapter 22: Discern the Voice of God

"My sheep listen to my voice; I know them, and they follow me."
—John 10:27

God Is Still Speaking But Are You Still Listening?

Some people think God has gone quiet. That He used to speak through burning bushes and booming clouds, but now He's gone silent. Absent. Distant.

But they're wrong.

God didn't lose His voice.

We lost our hearing.

Not because our ears broke. But because our lives got too loud.

We've filled every margin with something: music, scrolling, shows, podcasts, conversations, calendars. There's no silence left. No space.

And God's voice? It's still a whisper.

If you want to hear Him, you have to stop shouting.

If you want to listen, you have to get low.

"Be still, and know that I am God." (Psalm 46:10)

Stillness is the secret place where the whisper is heard.

When God Whispered to a Prophet

In 1 Kings 19, the prophet Elijah was worn out. Running for his life. Spiritually exhausted. Suicidal. He needed God to speak desperately.

God told him to stand on the mountain. And then came the wind... the earthquake... the fire.

But God wasn't in any of them.

Then a gentle whisper.

"And after the fire came a gentle whisper." (1 Kings 19:12)

Why whisper?

Because God was close.

God doesn't shout at His children. He draws them close and speaks in stillness.

If you can't hear Him, maybe it's not because He stopped talking. Maybe it's because you stopped sitting still long enough to listen.

Three Voices. One Choice.

Every day, you hear three voices:

The Voice of God – full of peace, truth, clarity, conviction, and grace.

The Voice of the Flesh – full of excuses, pride, compromise, and desire.

The Voice of the Enemy – full of fear, lies, accusation, and confusion.

Discernment is learning to know who's talking and deciding who gets the mic.

God's voice won't pressure you. It won't rush you. It won't shame you. It won't contradict Scripture. But it will call you higher. And it will always sound like Jesus.

What God's Voice Sounds Like

Don't overcomplicate it. Here's what to look for:

Biblical – It never contradicts Scripture.

Peaceful – Even when He corrects, peace follows.

Personal – It hits your heart like He's reading your journal.

Hopeful – Even His rebuke leads to life.

Convicting – It exposes darkness, not to shame you but to set you free.

If it draws you to repentance, stirs your faith, or moves you closer to Jesus then pay attention.

Barriers to Hearing His Voice

You can't hear a whisper if the noise never stops.

Ask yourself honestly:

Am I rushing through life without ever being still?

Is my phone the first voice I hear in the morning?

Am I numbing my spirit with constant entertainment?

Is there unrepented sin clouding my connection?

Do I even believe God still speaks?

These questions aren't to shame you. They're to help you get clear. Because clarity creates intimacy.

A Story from a Revival

In the Hebrides Revival (Scotland, late 1940s), two elderly sisters—one blind, one arthritic—prayed day and night for revival. One night, they sensed God say, "I will pour water on the thirsty land."

They didn't hear it audibly, but they knew. His whisper thundered in their spirits.

They called the local pastor. They gathered the people. And they waited.

Within weeks, the power of God fell.

People were gripped with repentance. Whole villages wept. Night after night, the Spirit drew people from their beds to the altars.

Why?

Because two women discerned the voice of God in prayer—and obeyed.

The whisper became a wildfire.

How to Tune In: Learning to Hear God's Voice

You won't hear Him by accident. It takes practice. But it's possible if you're intentional.

1. Be Still.
Find a quiet space. No phone. No agenda. Just you and Him.

"Be still, and know…" (Psalm 46:10)

2. Open His Word.
Read slowly. Listen between the lines. Ask, "God, what are You saying to me right now?"

"Your word is a lamp to my feet…" (Psalm 119:105)

3. Pray Honestly Then Wait.
Speak. Pause. Listen. Don't fill the silence. Let God answer.

"Call to me and I will answer you…" (Jeremiah 33:3)

4. Journal What You Sense.
Write it down. It helps you recognize patterns. See confirmations. Track growth.

5. Obey Quickly.

Every time you respond to God's whisper, His voice gets clearer. Every time you delay, it gets duller.

God Speaks in Many Ways

He's not limited.

Through Scripture (Hebrews 4:12)

Through the Holy Spirit (John 16:13)

Through wise believers (Proverbs 27:17)

Through dreams and visions (Acts 2:17)

Through nature (Romans 1:20)

Through your conscience (Romans 9:1)

Through circumstances (Romans 8:28)

But most of all He speaks in the secret place. Not to hide Himself, but to draw you near.

How to Know It's Not Just You

Ask these five questions:

Does it match God's Word?

Does it draw me closer to Jesus?

Does it encourage, convict, or comfort in truth?

Is it consistent with God's character?

Does it bear spiritual fruit?

If yes, step forward. If no, step back.

A Personal Moment

I once sat on the floor of my living room, asking God for direction on a big decision. No thunder. No angel. Just stillness.

Then a thought dropped into my spirit:
"It's not about the opportunity. It's about obedience."

I knew instantly. It wasn't my voice.

It sounded like peace.
It matched Scripture.
It aligned with His character.
It brought clarity.
It shifted everything.

That whisper saved me from a costly mistake.

The Closer You Walk, the Clearer He Sounds

Think of it like tuning a radio.

At first, there's static. Then a little clarity. Then—boom—crystal clear.

That's how it works with God.

Obey the last thing He said.

Stay in His Word.

Stay in His presence.

Stay hungry for His voice.

And soon, the whisper will become familiar.

You Were Created to Hear Him

This isn't for pastors, prophets, or "super Christians."

It's for you.

Jesus didn't say, "Some of My sheep hear Me."

He said:

"My sheep hear My voice; I know them, and they follow Me." (John 10:27)

That means if you're His, you can hear Him.

And when you do, follow Him. No hesitation. No delay.

Because obedience is the amplifier of intimacy.

One Thing to Remember

God is always speaking, but your spiritual hearing depends on your willingness to be still, listen, and obey.

One Step to Take

Set a timer for 10 minutes. Go to a quiet place. No phone. No music. Just prayer and silence. Then journal what you sense God saying.

One Scripture to Read Again

John 10:27
"My sheep listen to my voice; I know them, and they follow me."

Chapter 23: The Discipline of Holy Habits

"But I discipline my body and keep it under control, lest after preaching to others I myself should be disqualified."

—1 Corinthians 9:27

The Fire Won't Last Without Fuel

Revival doesn't come from emotion. It doesn't stay because of goosebumps or powerful music. It doesn't thrive just because you had a powerful encounter with God last week. The truth is, your spiritual fire fades when it's not fed—and it's only fed through discipline.

Paul, the same apostle who saw heaven, cast out demons, and walked in Holy Spirit power, still said, "I discipline my body and keep it under control." Why? Because he knew the fire inside of him could flicker if he didn't tend it.

You can't run a marathon off last month's meal. You can't fight a spiritual battle with last year's prayer life. God pours out fresh mercies every morning (Lamentations 3:22–23), not so we can coast—but so we'll come back daily to the source.

The hard truth? Passion without discipline burns out.

And many of us are burning out not because we lack love for God, but because we lack structure to protect and grow that love.

The Power of Small, Daily Choices

We often think of holy people as those who do big things—fast for 40 days, pray through the night, give away their life savings, or move to a foreign country. But holiness begins in the smallest daily choices.

Getting up 30 minutes early to read your Bible before work.

Turning off Netflix to spend time in prayer.

Pausing in the middle of a busy day to worship.

Saying no to a second helping to strengthen self-control.

Reaching out to a friend for spiritual accountability.

These things won't trend on Instagram. No one will give you a trophy. But God sees.

Jesus said, "Whoever is faithful with little will be entrusted with much" (Luke 16:10). If we want to carry revival, we must carry the habits that support it.

Why Discipline Feels So Hard

We love the fire of God until we realize we have to carry it in the rain. That's what discipline is—carrying fire through dry seasons, dull days, and dark valleys.

Our flesh hates routine. Our world loves comfort. Our culture preaches instant gratification.

But the kingdom of God is often counterintuitive:

You gain your life by losing it.

You lead by serving.

You grow strong by becoming weak.

You stay on fire by showing up daily, even when you don't feel it.

The enemy of your soul would rather you stay passionate and undisciplined than disciplined and devoted. Because passion without structure eventually turns to burnout. But disciplined devotion builds endurance, and endurance leads to maturity (James 1:4).

Holy Habits Are Not Legalism

Let's be clear: We are not saved by habits. We are not righteous because of routines. But discipline is the scaffolding that supports spiritual transformation.

The Pharisees had habits, but they lacked the heart. That's not what we're after.

God isn't calling you to robotic religion. He's calling you to a rhythm of relationship.

Think of habits as the garden fence. The fence doesn't make the fruit grow, but it protects the soil. When you build structure around your faith, you protect the flame God has placed inside you.

Discipline is not the enemy of grace. It's the vehicle that carries it.

A Glimpse Into Jesus' Rhythm

Jesus is our model. And even Jesus had habits.

"Very early in the morning, while it was still dark, Jesus got up, left the house and went off to a solitary place, where he prayed." (Mark 1:35)

"As was his custom, he went into the synagogue on the Sabbath day." (Luke 4:16)

"But Jesus often withdrew to lonely places and prayed." (Luke 5:16)

If Jesus, the Son of God, needed rhythm, structure, and discipline, how much more do we?

He didn't wing it. He didn't float through life waiting for a feeling. He set his alarm early, walked away from the crowds, and built a lifestyle that kept his heart connected to the Father.

So should we.

Building Your Own Holy Habit Plan

Here's how you can start. Don't wait for the perfect time. Start small. Stay consistent. Let grace cover your gaps.

Step 1: Choose One Habit

Don't try to do ten things. Choose one thing to build for the next 30 days. Some ideas:

Daily Bible reading (start with 10 minutes)

Morning prayer (even 5–10 minutes)

Worship music during your commute

Fasting one meal a week

Journaling your prayers every evening

Scripture memory (one verse a week)

Pick something that feels both challenging and achievable. You're not earning God's love. You're building a lifestyle that responds to it.

Step 2: Set a Time and Trigger

Habits stick when they're tied to something else you already do.

Examples:

"Right after I brush my teeth, I'll read one Psalm."

"Before I open social media, I'll pray the Lord's Prayer."

"As soon as I get into my car, I'll play one worship song."

Attach your habit to something concrete. That's how it moves from a wish to a rhythm.

Step 3: Track Your Progress

Don't obsess. But do track. Grab a calendar or checklist and mark each day you complete the habit.

It's not about perfection. It's about momentum.

But What If I Mess Up?

You will.

You'll miss a day. You'll forget. You'll fall asleep instead of praying. You'll eat the donut during your fast. You'll binge watch a show instead of reading Scripture.

You know what?

Grace is bigger than that.

Righteousness isn't about never falling. It's about getting up every time you do with God's help. Proverbs 24:16 says, "Though a righteous man falls seven times, he gets up again."

Don't let shame become your rhythm. Let repentance and reset become your rhythm.

God doesn't need your perfection. He wants your persistence.

Testimonies from the Trenches

Let me tell you about Carlos. Carlos was a new believer who tried to read his Bible for an hour every day and pray for 45 minutes before work. After three days, he gave up.

Then someone told him: "Start with five minutes. Just five."

So he did. Five minutes in the Psalms. Five minutes praying out loud. Day by day, week by week. It grew. One year later,

Carlos is a firebrand for Jesus, mentoring young men and fasting regularly. He'll tell you: it all started with five minutes.

Or Lisa. Lisa battled depression for years. She didn't have strength for long Bible studies or church events. But she made a habit of writing down one thing she was thankful for and praying one honest prayer each night before bed.

Now, she leads a prayer group and shares her testimony with women across her city.

It's not about grand gestures. It's about small, surrendered steps that build into spiritual strength.

One Thing to Remember

Your fire won't survive on emotion. It needs the structure of daily devotion. Holy habits protect your passion and carry you through the dry seasons.

One Step to Take

Choose one spiritual habit to commit to for the next 30 days. Write it down. Set a time. Track your progress. Tell a friend.

One Scripture to Read Again

1 Corinthians 9:27 – "But I discipline my body and keep it under control, lest after preaching to others I myself should be disqualified."

Chapter 24: Don't Grow Weary—The Harvest Is Coming

"Let us not grow weary in doing good, for at the proper time we will reap a harvest if we do not give up."

—Galatians 6:9

The Fire Fades If You Let It

You started strong. You were burning hot. You were waking up early, praying like never before, turning off distractions, fasting, giving, forgiving, and walking boldly in your faith. You were on fire.

But now?

Now you're tired. Quiet time feels dull. Prayers feel unanswered. People have disappointed you. Progress feels slow. Your passion isn't gone, but it's flickering. What once felt alive and fresh now feels like work.

You've hit the wall and the temptation to quit is strong.

But don't.

That wall you've hit? It's not the end. It's the test. It's where the enemy hopes you'll stop short. But God's Word says: Don't grow weary. Don't give up. The harvest is coming.

What If the Breakthrough Is Closer Than You Think?

Imagine a farmer who plows his fields, plants his seeds, waters the soil, and waits through a long season of silence. Then, right before the first sprout appears he walks away. Too tired. Too discouraged. Too impatient. He misses the harvest because he stopped too soon.

That's what many believers do.

We sow in prayer, in obedience, in faith. But when we don't see results right away, we grow weary. And when we grow weary, we grow vulnerable.

That's exactly when the enemy starts whispering:

"What's the point?"

"God's not listening."

"You're wasting your time."

"Go back to what's easy."

But hear this loud and clear: God's timing is not your timing, but He's never late. The harvest doesn't belong to the fast or the flashy. It belongs to the faithful.

"At the proper time we will reap a harvest if we do not give up." (Galatians 6:9)

Passion Is a Spark. Perseverance Is the Flame.

Passion will light the fire. But only perseverance will keep it burning.

The Bible never promises that following Jesus will always feel exciting. In fact, Jesus warned the exact opposite: "In this world, you will have trouble..." (John 16:33).

You will feel weary. You will face resistance. You will have days where you feel like nothing is working.

But God never calls you to live by feelings. He calls you to live by faith.

You can worship even when you don't feel it. You can pray when it feels dry. You can serve when it's unnoticed. You can love when it's hard.

That's spiritual maturity not chasing mountaintop emotions, but choosing to stay faithful in the valley.

Look at Jesus.

Our Savior didn't quit. He didn't stop halfway. He didn't walk away when it got hard. He endured.

Betrayed by friends.

Mocked by crowds.

Beaten, bloodied, and nailed to a cross.

Yet He stayed faithful, because of the joy set before Him (Hebrews 12:2).

What was the joy?

You.

Your salvation. Your freedom. Your eternity.

Jesus didn't grow weary. He didn't give up. And now, through His Spirit, you don't have to either.

You carry the same Spirit that raised Christ from the dead (Romans 8:11). That means you carry resurrection power in your weakness. You don't have to manufacture strength. You have to stay connected to the Source.

How to Keep Going When You're Tired

Let's get practical. When your spiritual gas tank is running low, here's how to refuel:

1. Return to the Why

Why did you start following Jesus in the first place? Was it to feel good? Or was it because you knew He was the only one who could save you?

Go back to the cross. Go back to your first love. Remember what He's done. Remember who you were. Remember how far He's brought you.

2. Rest, Don't Quit

Sometimes what you need isn't to give up, but to pull back and rest.

Even Jesus rested. He stepped away from crowds. He went off by Himself to pray. He slept in the boat during the storm. Why? Because rest isn't weakness. It's wisdom.

Take a break from performance, not from presence. Stop trying to impress people. Sit with God. Let Him refill you.

3. Speak the Word Out Loud

When you're under attack, your mouth becomes a weapon.

Say this when you're weary:

"I can do all things through Christ who strengthens me." (Philippians 4:13)

"The Lord is my shepherd; I lack nothing." (Psalm 23:1)

"The joy of the Lord is my strength." (Nehemiah 8:10)

"I will reap a harvest if I do not give up." (Galatians 6:9)

You don't need to feel strong to declare truth. Say it until your soul believes it again.

4. Let Someone In

Don't suffer in silence. Tell a friend, pastor, or mentor: "I'm weary. I'm fighting to stay faithful."

You're not weak for needing help. You're wise. The enemy wants to isolate you. God wants to strengthen you in community.

A Word for the Weary

There's someone reading this who's ready to give up.

You're discouraged. Tired. Overwhelmed. You've been doing the right things, but the results feel invisible.

Hear me:

God sees you.
God is with you.
And God is not done.

The harvest is coming. But it won't come to the quitter. It comes to the one who keeps sowing, keeps praying, keeps walking, and keeps trusting even when it's hard.

Galatians 6:9 isn't a suggestion. It's a lifeline: "Let us not grow weary in doing good, for at the proper time we will reap a harvest if we do not give up."

Faithfulness Is the Firewood of Revival

Do you want to live on fire for Jesus? Then build your life with long obedience. Don't chase spiritual highs. Build holy habits. Live with discipline. Stay connected to the Word. Keep showing up.

That's how revival is sustained.

God doesn't anoint perfect people. He anoints surrendered ones. Consistent ones. Persevering ones.

You're Closer Than You Think

The devil knows your harvest is near. That's why he's turning up the heat. That's why the attacks feel heavier. That's why the thoughts of quitting have gotten louder.

Don't fall for it.

You might be one prayer away from breakthrough. One more week from healing. One more act of obedience from seeing the door open.

This is not the time to give up.

This is the time to press in.

What You Sow Now, You'll Reap Later

You won't always see the fruit right away.

You read the Bible and feel nothing.

You pray and the answers seem delayed.

You love that difficult person and they don't change.

You fast and the breakthrough hasn't come.

But behind the scenes, God is working.

Your obedience is planting seeds. Seeds of faith. Seeds of hope. Seeds of power. Seeds of healing.

And God promises you will reap. IF you don't give up.

That's the condition. That's the key.

One Thing to Remember

Passion may get you started, but perseverance gets you across the finish line. Don't quit. Your harvest is coming.

One Step to Take

Write down one spiritual commitment you won't quit, even when you're tired. Tape it somewhere you'll see it every day. Let it anchor your soul when the feelings fade.

One Scripture to Read Again

Galatians 6:9 – "Let us not grow weary in doing good, for at the proper time we will reap a harvest if we do not give up."

Chapter 25: Be the Alarm in a World Asleep

"But if the watchman sees the sword coming and does not blow the trumpet to warn the people... I will hold the watchman accountable."

–Ezekiel 33:6

The World Is Asleep

Look around you.

We live in a world asleep to eternity. People chase money, entertainment, popularity, and comfort, but they forget God. They scroll all day and sleepwalk through life. Their eyes are open, but their souls are closed.

And too often, so are ours.

Too often, Christians are quiet when they should speak. We get comfortable in the crowd. We tone it down so we don't offend. We blend in when we were made to stand out.

But this is not the time to go quiet. This is not the time to blend in.

This is the time to wake people up.

You are the alarm God wants to sound.

You're Not Just Saved: You're Sent

When Jesus saved you, He didn't just rescue you. He recruited you.

He didn't just forgive your sins. He commissioned you to help others be forgiven too.

Christianity is not a private belief system for people to keep to themselves. It is a bold, public invitation to leave darkness and walk into light.

You are not just a believer. You are a watchman.

In Ezekiel 33, God told His prophet, "If the watchman sees the sword coming and does not blow the trumpet to warn the people... I will hold the watchman accountable."

That sounds heavy. And it is.

Because God has placed people in your life for a reason. Family. Friends. Coworkers. Neighbors. Classmates. Teammates.

You may be the only alarm they ever hear.

Being an Alarm Isn't Always Easy

Let's be honest. Sharing your faith is scary.

You might worry:

"What if they think I'm weird?"

"What if they ask a question I can't answer?"

"What if I ruin the relationship?"

"What if I say the wrong thing?"

But let me ask a deeper question:

What if you stay silent—and they never get another chance?

Hell is real. Eternity is forever. Souls are on the line.

Would you rather feel awkward for 30 seconds—or regretful for eternity?

When God gives you the nudge to speak, don't silence it. Speak up. Share what He's done. Invite them to church. Ask how you can pray for them. Offer hope.

You don't have to preach a sermon. You just have to tell your story and point them to Jesus.

Wake Up and Walk Boldly

God isn't looking for perfect people to speak up. He's looking for available ones. Willing ones. People who say, "Here I am, Lord. Send me."

If you're still breathing, you're still on assignment.

This generation doesn't need more influencers. They need more intercessors. They don't need more opinions. They need truth. They don't need more noise. They need the alarm.

You may think your voice doesn't matter. But it does.

When you speak up, you become a trumpet in God's hands.

How to Be the Alarm

If you want to sound the alarm in a world asleep, here's how:

1. Wake Up First

You can't wake others up if you're still half asleep yourself.

This entire book has been leading to this point: You can't call others to the fire if you haven't stepped into it yourself.

Get on your knees. Get in the Word. Get honest. Let the Holy Spirit refine you. When people see your life burning bright, they'll want to know the Source of the fire.

Revival starts in you before it spreads through you.

2. Pray With Targeted Fire

Don't just pray for the world in general. Start with three specific people you know who need Jesus. Write their names down. Ask God to soften their hearts. Ask Him to open a door for conversation. Ask Him to use you.

Then pray daily. Call their names out to heaven.

Spiritual battles are not won with opinions. They're won on your knees.

3. Share Your Testimony

You don't need a Bible degree to be a witness. You just need a story. And if you've met Jesus, you have one.

Tell someone:

Who you were before Christ.

How you encountered Him.

Who you are now.

People may argue theology. But they can't argue with a changed life.

Your testimony is someone else's wake-up call.

4. Invite Boldly

Start inviting people into what God is doing.

Invite them to:

Church.

A Bible study.

A worship night.

Your home for a meal and spiritual conversation.

It doesn't have to be polished. Just be real.

Don't underestimate the power of an invitation. Eternity may change because you opened your mouth.

You Are the Trumpet in God's Hand

In the Old Testament, when the people of God were in danger, watchmen stood on the walls and blew the trumpet. That sound meant wake up, get ready, take action.

You are that trumpet now.

Every word you speak in love… every conversation you risk… every time you invite someone to know Jesus… you are sounding the alarm.

And someone's life may depend on it.

You are not here to blend in. You are here to wake the world up.

But What If They Reject Me?

They might.

They might laugh. They might ignore you. They might roll their eyes or change the subject.

But listen carefully: It's not your job to save people. It's your job to speak.

Jesus said, "If the world hates you, keep in mind that it hated me first." (John 15:18)

Rejection is not failure. Silence is.

If they walk away from your message, let it be because they rejected the truth, not because they never heard it.

You Were Made for This

You weren't born in this generation by accident. You're not in your school, job, family, or city by chance.

God placed you here. Now. On purpose. For a purpose.

And part of that purpose is to be His mouthpiece.

Let your life echo the love of Jesus. Let your story shout redemption. Let your courage stir conviction. Let your words open blind eyes.

You are not invisible. You are not powerless.

You are the alarm. Sound it.

One Thing to Remember

God isn't asking you to be perfect. He's asking you to be bold. Sound the alarm. Someone's eternity may depend on it.

One Step to Take

Pray for three people by name. Ask God to give you an open door this week to reach out, share your story, or simply offer hope. Then take the step even if your voice shakes.

One Scripture to Read Again

Ezekiel 33:6 – "But if the watchman sees the sword coming and does not blow the trumpet to warn the people… I will hold the watchman accountable."

Chapter 26: Tell Your Story, Even If It's Messy

"They triumphed over him by the blood of the Lamb and by the word of their testimony…"

- Revelation 12:11

The Power in Your Story

You may not feel like a preacher. You may not see yourself as someone God could use to impact lives. But if you have been saved by Jesus Christ, you carry something that hell fears:

Your story.

Your testimony is not just a nice story of personal growth. It's a weapon.

Revelation 12:11 doesn't say we overcome Satan by perfect behavior or fancy theology. It says we overcome him "by the blood of the Lamb and by the word of our testimony."

There is power in your story. And when you open your mouth to share it, the devil loses ground.

But the enemy's goal is to keep you silent.

He whispers lies like:

"Your story isn't dramatic enough."

"It's too messy. Don't bring that up."

"You've failed too many times."

"Nobody wants to hear from you."

Don't believe it. That's fear talking, not faith.

If Jesus saved you, you have a testimony. And someone needs to hear it.

Even the Messy Parts Matter

Most people don't relate to perfection. They relate to pain. They don't connect with polished religion. They connect with real redemption.

God doesn't just use our strength. He uses our scars.

The very parts of your story you're tempted to hide might be the exact parts God wants to highlight to reach someone else. Your brokenness may be someone else's breakthrough.

Think about it:

That addiction you fought through? Someone else is fighting it now.

That shame you carried? Someone else is still carrying it.

That dark season where you felt hopeless? Someone else is there now, praying for light.

Your testimony is proof that Jesus still saves. That He still restores. That He still heals. That He still changes lives.

And when you tell it, even in its messiness, you shine light into someone else's darkness.

Don't Wait Until You're "Ready"

Some people think, "I'll share my story once I've got it all figured out."

But here's the truth: God doesn't need you to be finished to use you. He needs you to be faithful.

The woman at the well in John 4 didn't wait for Bible school. She didn't wait to fix her reputation. She ran into town right after meeting Jesus and told everyone what had happened.

And many in that town believed because of her testimony.

She didn't clean herself up first. She just said, "Come meet a man who told me everything I ever did. Could He be the Messiah?"

That's it.

Simple. Honest. Messy.

But it changed lives.

Yours can too.

What's in a Testimony?

You don't need to write a novel. You need three minutes.

Here's a simple structure:

1. Before Christ

What was your life like before you met Jesus?

What did you chase?

What did you struggle with?

What was missing?

This isn't about glorifying sin, but being honest about the emptiness and need that led you to Him.

2. Meeting Christ

How did Jesus become real to you?

Was there a moment?

A process?

What finally clicked?

This is the turning point. Talk about how your eyes opened, your heart softened, and your life shifted.

3. After Christ

What has changed?

How has your thinking shifted?

How has God moved in your heart?

What's still hard, but now filled with hope?

Let them see that you're not perfect, but you're different.

Your Story Unlocks Someone Else's Cage

Think of Paul.

He had a wild testimony. Murdered Christians. Hated Jesus. Then God showed up, blinded him, changed him, and used him to write half the New Testament.

And what did Paul keep doing, over and over again?

He told his story.

In Acts 22, he shares it with a hostile crowd. In Acts 26, he shares it with a king. Over and over, Paul uses the same story to lead people to Christ.

And that story still echoes 2,000 years later.

Your story may not be dramatic, but it's divinely assigned. God chose you. And your words could unlock chains for someone else.

You Never Know Who's Listening

A few words can change eternity.

I once heard about a man who got invited to a church service by a friend he barely knew. He went out of politeness. He sat in the back row. He had no plans to respond.

But one person stood up and told their story.

They talked about growing up in church but never really knowing Jesus. They talked about drifting, doubting, and coming back. It was raw and real.

And that man in the back row? He couldn't stop the tears. Because that was his story too.

That night, he gave his life to Jesus.

All because someone was brave enough to tell their story.

Don't Dress It Up: Just Tell It

You don't need fancy words.

You don't need to sound like a preacher.

You don't need to explain everything perfectly.

You just need to be honest.

When you speak from the heart, God takes your words and does something supernatural. It's not about what you say. It's about the Holy Spirit moving through it.

God will use your courage more than your eloquence.

Action: Write Your 3-Minute Testimony

Take a moment right now to write out your testimony.

Don't overthink it. Just answer the three big questions:

What was your life like before Jesus?

How did you come to know Him?

How has your life changed since?

If you're not sure what to say, just imagine you're sitting across the table from someone who's hurting. What would you want them to know?

Start there.

Then pray this simple prayer:

"Lord, use my story for Your glory. Let it reach the ears that need to hear it. Give me courage to speak, even when I'm nervous. And let someone's eternity change because I was willing to share."

One Thing to Remember

Your story, even the messy parts, can lead someone else to freedom. Don't hide what God wants to use.

One Step to Take

Write your 3-minute testimony today. Then ask God to show you one person to share it with this week. Don't delay. The time is now.

One Scripture to Read Again

Revelation 12:11 – "They triumphed over him by the blood of the Lamb and by the word of their testimony…"

Chapter 27: Live Like Eternity Is Real

"So we fix our eyes not on what is seen, but on what is unseen, since what is seen is temporary, but what is unseen is eternal."

–2 Corinthians 4:18

This Isn't All There Is

Let's cut straight to the point.

You are going to die.

That's not fear-mongering. It's a fact. One hundred percent of people eventually leave this life. The question isn't if, but then what?

The Apostle Paul wrote that the things we see are temporary. What really matters—what truly lasts—is unseen. Eternal.

But you wouldn't know that by watching how most people live. We chase money like it'll matter forever. We cling to comfort like it's our god. We argue over opinions while souls around us are drowning.

Most people are sprinting toward the grave with their eyes shut.

But friend, eternity is real.

And once you see it, you can't go back to pretending this world is all there is.

Eternity Isn't a Concept: It's a Reality

Eternity isn't poetic language. It's not a vague cloud in the sky or a metaphor for something nice.

It's a timeline that never ends.

Imagine this: stretch out a rope from one end of the earth to the other. Now put a dot on the first inch of that rope. That dot is your life on earth. The rest is eternity.

What you do with that dot determines where and how you spend the rest of the rope.

Jesus said in Matthew 7:13–14:

"Enter through the narrow gate. For wide is the gate and broad is the road that leads to destruction, and many enter through it. But small is the gate and narrow the road that leads to life, and only a few find it."

Most people are not on the road to Heaven. That's what Jesus said. Only a few are.

And if that's true, then we cannot afford to drift through life distracted by what doesn't matter.

Wake Up to What's Coming

Heaven is real. Hell is real. And Jesus talked more about Hell than anyone else in Scripture, not because He wanted to scare people, but because He wanted to rescue them.

You might think:

"But I'm a good person."

"I go to church sometimes."

"I try to be kind."

That's not salvation.

Salvation is surrender. It's putting your full trust in Jesus Christ alone for forgiveness and eternal life. Nothing else will hold up when eternity comes knocking.

Hebrews 9:27 says:

"It is appointed unto man once to die, and after this comes judgment."

There is no reincarnation. No second chance. No do-over. Once this life ends, the next begins.

And there are only two doors.

One opens to life with God forever: more beautiful, thrilling, joyful, and holy than anything we can imagine. The other opens to separation from God: painful, dark, and final.

The good news? You don't have to guess where you'll go. Jesus made a way. And you can know Him today.

What If We Really Believed This?

Let's stop for a moment.

If you truly believed that Heaven and Hell were real, that souls were hanging in the balance, and that this life is just a blink—how would it change you?

Would you:

Forgive faster?

Love deeper?

Pray bolder?

Share your faith more often?

Spend your time differently?

The early church turned the world upside down because they lived with eternity in view.

Paul could take beatings, shipwrecks, betrayals, and prison because he saw through the lens of forever.

He said in Romans 8:18:

"I consider that our present sufferings are not worth comparing with the glory that will be revealed in us."

They lived for the eternal, not the earthly.

So must we.

Temporary Things Lose Their Grip

When your eyes are fixed on eternity, the things that once seemed so important start to lose their hold.

That insult? It's temporary.

That promotion you didn't get? Temporary.

That house, that car, that status? All temporary.

But what isn't temporary?

The soul of your neighbor.

The prayers you prayed in secret.

The quiet obedience that no one applauded.

The moments you shared Jesus with trembling hands and a burning heart.

Those things will echo in eternity.

You cannot take your bank account, your reputation, or your trophies with you. But you can take people.

Live for what lasts.

Don't Let the Devil Lull You to Sleep

One of Satan's favorite lies is: "You have time."

He won't tell you there's no God. He'll just whisper, "You can get serious later."

He wants you to believe the lie of someday, that you'll follow Jesus fully once you're older, or less busy, or more settled.

But someday is not promised.

James 4:14 says:

"You are a mist that appears for a little while and then vanishes."

Your life is a vapor. Here, then gone.

If you're reading this, that means God has given you another day. Another chance.

Don't waste it.

Live Now Like You'll Stand Before Him Soon

You will stand before Jesus.

Face to face.

Eyes that burn with holiness. Hands that still bear the scars. Voice like many waters.

He will not ask how popular you were.

He will not care about your social media following.

He will not reward the size of your house.

He will look at your heart, your obedience, and your love for Him.

Will you hear, "Well done, good and faithful servant"?

Or will you hear, "Depart from Me, I never knew you"?

This isn't meant to scare you. It's meant to wake you up.

Because nothing matters more than being ready for that moment.

Action: Visualize Eternity for One Week

Let's make this practical.

For the next seven days, take five minutes each day and visualize eternity.

Ask yourself:

What will matter 100 years from now?

How am I living for that?

What needs to shift?

Use a journal. Use a note on your phone. But reflect. Pray. Let the Holy Spirit speak.

Here's a short prayer to guide you each morning:

"Lord, help me live today like eternity is real. Open my eyes. Set my priorities. Let me invest in what will last forever."

You may be shocked at how your decisions, conversations, and desires begin to shift.

One Thing to Remember

Eternity is real. Live now like you'll stand before Jesus soon, because you will.

One Step to Take

Visualize eternity for five minutes a day over the next seven days. Let it reset your values and ignite your urgency.

One Scripture to Read Again

2 Corinthians 4:18 – "So we fix our eyes not on what is seen, but on what is unseen, since what is seen is temporary, but what is unseen is eternal."

Chapter 28: Watch and Pray

"Watch and pray so that you will not fall into temptation. The spirit is willing, but the flesh is weak."

–Matthew 26:41

The Final Hour Demands a Final Wake-Up

Let me ask you a serious question: Are you watching, or are you sleeping?

Jesus didn't say this to the crowds. He didn't shout it to the Pharisees. He spoke it quietly, almost heartbreakingly, to His closest friends—in the garden, just before He was betrayed.

"Watch and pray," He told them, "so that you will not fall into temptation."

But what did they do?

They fell asleep.

Not once. Not twice. Three times.

And before we judge them too quickly, let's look in the mirror.

How often has the Lord called us to wake up and we've hit snooze? How often has He whispered, Come away with Me. Seek My face. But we rolled over and kept scrolling?

The hour is late.

We are not waiting for the end times to come. We are living in them.

Now is not the time for spiritual sleep. It's time to watch and pray.

What Does It Mean to Watch?

Watching in Scripture is not passive.

It's not sitting on your couch looking out the window, hoping Jesus taps you on the shoulder when He arrives.

To watch is to be alert, spiritually awake, eyes wide open to the reality of what's happening in the world and what's happening in your heart.

Jesus told His disciples to watch because danger was near. And He tells us the same.

1 Peter 5:8 warns:

"Be sober-minded; be watchful. Your adversary the devil prowls around like a roaring lion, seeking someone to devour."

The devil doesn't take naps. The kingdom of darkness doesn't go on vacation. Why do we think we can live spiritually lazy lives and expect to stand firm?

We need a church that's watching—not just for headlines and signs of the times, but for attacks on our souls and the souls of others.

Are you watching?

Or are you numb, distracted, or indifferent?

The Second Half: Pray

Jesus didn't just say "watch." He said, "Watch and pray."

Why?

Because watching without praying leads to worry.

But watching with prayer leads to power.

Prayer is not just a nice spiritual practice. It's war. It's a weapon. It's the very air your spirit breathes.

When you pray, you're not talking to the ceiling. You're entering the throne room of the Most High. You're aligning heaven with earth. You're shaking the gates of hell. You're interceding for the souls of others.

That's why the devil works so hard to keep you from it.

He knows a praying believer is dangerous. A prayerless one is asleep at the wheel.

The Garden Test

Let's go back to the Garden of Gethsemane.

Jesus was fully God, but also fully man, and in that moment He was in agony. He asked His closest friends to stay with Him, to pray, to watch. And what did He find when He came back?

"Could you not keep watch with Me for one hour?"

What a question.

What if Jesus is still asking us that today?

Could you not turn off your phone and pray for your family?

Could you not stay awake and fight for your city?

Could you not get up early and seek My face?

We fail the garden test when we forget what's at stake.

But here's the grace: He calls us again.

Prayer Keeps You Ready

You want to live on fire? Then you need firepower, and that comes through prayer.

You can read every book. Attend every church service. Quote Scripture from memory.

But if you do not pray, if you do not abide in Him, you will burn out.

Jesus said in John 15:5:

"Apart from Me, you can do nothing."

Not "some things."

Nothing.

Prayer isn't optional. It's survival.

It keeps your heart soft. It opens your ears. It clears the fog. It stokes the fire.

Without it, you'll drift. With it, you'll soar.

Intercession: Carrying the Burden for Others

One of the greatest ways to "sound the alarm" in this world is to pray for others, to stand in the gap, to lift them up, to fight for their souls in the spirit.

That's called intercession.

Ezekiel 22:30 says:

"I looked for someone among them who would build up the wall and stand before Me in the gap on behalf of the land so I would not have to destroy it, but I found no one."

Don't let that be said of your generation.

Be the one who stands in the gap. Be the one who lifts up a friend's name, a prodigal child, a wayward spouse, a lost neighbor.

Prayer changes things.

Moses' intercession saved Israel from destruction. Esther's fasting and prayer saved a nation. Paul's prayers shook prison walls. And Jesus Himself still lives to intercede for us (Hebrews 7:25).

Do not underestimate what happens when you pray.

How to Build a Prayer Rhythm

If you don't schedule prayer, you'll skip prayer.

Life will always be full. But prayer isn't something we do when we have time. It's something we make time for.

Here's a simple structure to get you started:

1. Set a time.

Pick a consistent time—morning, lunch, evening—whatever works best. Even 15 minutes is powerful.

2. Pick a place.

Create a space that feels like a "meeting place" with God. It could be your bedroom, a prayer chair, a corner with a journal.

3. Start with worship.

Play a worship song. Read a Psalm. Lift your heart before lifting your requests.

4. Pray Scripture.

Open your Bible. Let the Word guide your prayers. Personalize verses into prayers.

Example: "Lord, help me fix my eyes not on what is seen, but on what is unseen..."

5. Pray for others.

Make a list. Pray for them by name. Be specific.

6. Listen.

Don't just talk. Be still. Let the Lord speak. Journal what you hear.

A Generation on Its Knees

Do you know what this world is waiting for?

Not more influencers. Not louder opinions. Not bigger buildings.

It's waiting for a church on its knees.

A praying church is a powerful church.

A praying family is a protected family.

A praying believer is a burning believer.

Let the revival you're longing for begin with your prayer life.

Action: Build a Rhythm of Intercessory Prayer

You were born for this.

Not to sleep through the storm but to rise with holy alertness.

This week, build your rhythm.

Here's a challenge:

Day 1: Write out a prayer list of five people who need Jesus.

Day 2: Set a time and place for daily prayer.

Day 3: Pray aloud using Scripture.

Day 4: Intercede for your family and your church.

Day 5: Ask God to show you someone hurting and pray for them.

Day 6: Spend five minutes listening and journaling.

Day 7: Worship and thank Him for what you can't yet see.

Repeat. Build the rhythm. Watch what God does.

One Thing to Remember

Prayer isn't passive: it's power. Jesus didn't say watch or pray. He said, watch and pray.

One Step to Take

Build a daily rhythm of intercessory prayer. Start this week.

One Scripture to Read Again

Matthew 26:41 – "Watch and pray so that you will not fall into temptation. The spirit is willing, but the flesh is weak."

Chapter 29: The Trumpet Will Sound

"For the Lord himself will come down from heaven, with a loud command, with the voice of the archangel and with the trumpet call of God, and the dead in Christ will rise first. After that, we who are still alive and are left will be caught up together with them in the clouds to meet the Lord in the air. And so we will be with the Lord forever."

—1 Thessalonians 4:16-17 (NIV)

The Sky Will Split. The Earth Will Tremble. Eternity Will Begin.

There is coming a day unlike any day the world has ever known.

No warning. No countdown. No rescheduling.

The sky will rip open. A trumpet will echo across every nation, every ocean, every mountain, and every hidden valley. The dead in Christ will rise. And the Son of God, no longer in a manger, no longer wearing a crown of thorns, will descend in unimaginable glory.

It won't be a dream.

It won't be a myth.

It won't be a metaphor.

It will be the most real, raw, undeniable moment in the history of the universe.

And in that split second, every soul will stand before one question:
Was I ready?

A Personal Story: The Fire Drill That Wasn't

I remember once, during my childhood, we had a surprise fire drill at school. But this time, it wasn't announced over the PA system. The alarms blared without warning. Students panicked. Teachers scrambled. And amidst the confusion, we realized something profound: most of us didn't know what to do because we weren't actually ready. We only thought we were.

That's how it will be when the trumpet sounds.

Only this time, it won't be a drill.

The Last Sound You'll Ever Hear on Earth

When Paul wrote to the Thessalonian believers, he wasn't trying to craft a dramatic speech. He was preparing the Church for the moment that ends time as we know it. This wasn't about curiosity or controversy. It was about urgency.

The trumpet Paul describes won't be an angelic background soundtrack. It will be the sound of finality. Of fulfilled prophecy. Of heaven invading earth.

And whether you are driving on the highway, working in your office, scrolling your phone, or fast asleep, it will come.

Like lightning.

Like a thief in the night.

Like a tidal wave that doesn't wait for permission.

A Glimpse from History: The Great Lisbon Earthquake

On November 1, 1755, a massive earthquake struck Lisbon, Portugal. It was sudden. Violent. And within minutes, thousands were dead. Churches collapsed. Fires consumed the city. Tidal waves followed. People thought it was Judgment Day.

Some ran to the altars.

Others cursed God.

And some, frozen in terror, simply waited to die.

If one natural disaster could provoke that much fear and chaos, imagine the moment when Jesus returns, not to shake a city, but to shake the cosmos.

This time, it won't be a rehearsal. It will be the reckoning.

The Return of the King

Jesus came once to save the world.

He is coming again to judge it.

"Look, he is coming with the clouds," Revelation 1:7 says, "and every eye will see him, even those who pierced him; and all peoples on earth will mourn because of him."

To the faithful, it will be a long-awaited homecoming.

To the unrepentant, it will be the collapse of every excuse, every argument, every delay.

Don't Be the One Who Waited Too Long

Picture this: A man sits in his living room. The news is on. Chaos unfolds. Reports pour in about people vanishing. Planes crashing. Families separated. Mass hysteria.

And this man who had every opportunity to surrender, every sermon in his memory, every chance to repent now weeps in unspeakable regret.

He remembers the whispers. The altar calls. The friend who pleaded with him.

And he realizes he's not just living through a crisis.

He missed the Christ.

The Trumpet Will Separate the Committed from the Casual

There won't be categories.

Just two responses:

For some, the trumpet will be the sweetest sound they've ever heard.

For others, it will be the saddest sound they'll never forget.

"Then two men will be in the field; one will be taken and one left." (Matthew 24:40)

There is no neutral when Jesus returns. No second chances. No negotiating. No hiding behind someone else's faith.

What Readiness Looks Like

Readiness isn't about being perfect. It's about being prepared.

It's not about religious activity. It's about relationship.

It's about a life aligned with eternity, where your oil is full, your hands are clean, and your heart is fixed on Heaven.

"Therefore keep watch," Jesus said, "because you do not know on what day your Lord will come." (Matthew 24:42)

Readiness is...

Praying with hunger, not obligation.

Loving His appearing, not fearing it.

Living like your life is not your own.

Keeping your lamp burning when others let theirs go out.

A Wake-Up Call for the Church

The early Church believed Jesus could return any moment. That belief fueled their boldness.

They weren't trying to be impressive. They were trying to be obedient. They weren't building platforms. They were preparing people.

But somewhere along the way, the Church got sleepy. Comfortable. Distracted. Entertained.

We stopped watching. We stopped longing. We stopped warning.

But the trumpet hasn't stopped preparing to sound.

The Revival Before the Return

In the Welsh Revival of 1904, entire towns shut down to seek the Lord. Taverns emptied. Churches overflowed. Crime rates dropped. People wept in the streets not from fear, but from conviction. Why?

Because the fear of the Lord fell and with it, the desire to be ready.

This is the revival we need again.

Not just one of emotion. But one of urgency. One of holiness. One of people crying out, "Lord, come quickly—and find me faithful."

One Final Moment. One Eternal Outcome.

When the trumpet sounds, you won't have time to repent. To reconcile. To decide.

The time for that is now.

Because when the King returns, His eyes will be flames. His voice like rushing waters. His presence so holy the nations will tremble.

He's not coming for the crowd. He's coming for the Bride.

And not a lukewarm bride.
A radiant one.
A faithful one.
A ready one.

Let Your Life Be the Trumpet

You don't just wait for His coming. You warn others of it.

You don't just anticipate eternity. You prepare people for it.

So let your life sound the alarm.

Let your words point to Jesus.

Let your actions declare the urgency.

Because one day, the trumpet will sound in the sky.

But today, it must sound in your heart.

One Thing to Remember
Jesus is coming back. Not as a rumor, but as a reality. Not quietly, but with a trumpet. Not someday, but soon.

One Step to Take
Write a letter to your future self the day after Jesus returns. What will matter then? Who will you wish you had told? What will you wish you had left behind or picked up? Let it reset your life today.

One Scripture to Read Again

1 Thessalonians 4:16–17

"For the Lord Himself will descend from heaven with a shout, with the voice of an archangel, and with the trumpet of God. And the dead in Christ will rise first. Then we who are alive and remain shall be caught up together with them in the clouds to meet the Lord in the air. And thus we shall always be with the Lord."

Chapter 30: Your Fire Can Spark a Revival

"They saw what seemed to be tongues of fire that separated and came to rest on each of them. All of them were filled with the Holy Spirit and began to speak in other tongues as the Spirit enabled them."

- Acts 2:3-4

The Flame That Changed Everything

It didn't start in a cathedral.
It didn't begin with a famous preacher, an Instagram post, or a massive worship tour.

It began in an upper room.
With 120 people.
Waiting.
Praying.
Desperate.

They didn't know exactly what would happen. They just knew Jesus told them to stay. To wait for the Promise. And then it happened.

A sound like a violent wind rushed in. Tongues of fire appeared. Heaven came down and rested not on a select few, not just on Peter or John, but on every single person in the room. Fishermen, women, tax collectors, ordinary folks. The Holy Spirit filled them, and suddenly, weak people became bold witnesses. Scared disciples became fearless apostles.

And with one spark, revival ignited.

A Personal Fire with a Global Impact

You might feel small.
Insignificant.
Invisible even.

But you are not.
Heaven sees you. And when Heaven lights a fire in your soul, Hell trembles.

Don't underestimate what God can do through your life. Your "yes" to Him today can ripple through generations. One surrendered life is all it takes.

Let me tell you about Delia Knox.

She was paralyzed in a car accident and confined to a wheelchair for over 20 years. She worshiped from that chair, prayed from that chair, and believed God from that chair. At a revival service in Mobile, Alabama in 2010, during extended worship and ministry, Delia suddenly felt strength return to her legs. Supported by others, she stood for the first time in over two decades. She began walking. Worship turned into weeping. That moment of revival didn't just change Delia's life, it restored the faith of thousands watching.

Revival is deeply personal. But it never stays private.

The Pattern of Fire

From Genesis to Revelation, fire is a marker of God's presence:

God spoke to Moses through a burning bush that never burned out.

Fire fell from Heaven on Elijah's altar as proof that Yahweh was the true God.

Jesus promised a baptism "with the Holy Spirit and with fire" (Matthew 3:11).

And in Acts 2, fire didn't just descend from Heaven. It divided and rested on each one.

That detail matters.

Revival fire is not corporate before it's personal. It doesn't rest on buildings. It rests on people. On you.

You Are the Matchstick

God often chooses the ones the world overlooks. The ones still wrestling with insecurity, shame, or doubt. The woman at the well had five failed marriages—but her testimony sparked revival in Samaria. The demoniac in the Gerasenes was a spiritual outcast, but after one encounter with Jesus, he became the first missionary to the Decapolis.

And maybe you've felt unqualified, too.

Maybe your past is messy.
Maybe your prayer life feels dry.
Maybe you've tried before and fallen hard.

Good.

God loves using people who have nothing to prove and everything to surrender. You're not the fire. You're the matchstick. But when you let Him strike, everything changes.

History Bends When People Burn

Revival is not a myth. It's not a dream from the past. It's a holy reality that keeps reappearing when God finds people hungry enough to host it.

Let's look at a few stories:

The First Great Awakening (1730s–1740s):
Jonathan Edwards preached a sermon titled Sinners in the Hands of an Angry God, and people literally clung to the

wooden pews, weeping in repentance. Churches filled. Taverns emptied. America shifted.

The Hebrides Revival (1949):
On a small island off the coast of Scotland, two elderly sisters, Peggy and Christine Smith, began praying. They couldn't leave their house, but their prayers reached Heaven. Within weeks, the Spirit fell on the entire island. Services ran through the night. People repented in the streets. No advertising. Just glory.

The Asbury Outpouring (2023):
A simple chapel service at Asbury University in Kentucky turned into 16 days of nonstop worship, prayer, and repentance. Students skipped class to kneel at the altar. Worship never stopped. Social media didn't spark it. It only spread it. The hunger was real. And it reminded the world: God is still moving.

These revivals didn't begin with stages. They began with surrender.

The Fuel of Revival

Let's be honest. Fire doesn't just fall. It's attracted to sacrifice.

Here's what revival fire needs:

Surrender – Revival starts when you finally stop trying to control God and start letting Him control you.

Repentance – Not just regret. Not just feeling bad. Repentance that turns your heart, your habits, your whole direction back toward Jesus.

Unity – The upper room was filled with people who were "of one accord." Revival won't fall on a divided house.

Intercession – Revival is born in prayer closets before it is seen on platforms. If you want revival in your city, birth it on your knees.

Light the Torch in Your Circle

Revival starts where you are.

It starts when you gather your kids and pray with them even when it feels awkward.

It starts when you turn off the TV and open your Bible instead.

It starts when you invite your coworkers to pray over lunch even if they say no.

It starts when you speak boldly about Jesus when everything inside you wants to stay quiet.

And if someone else lights up because of your obedience? Praise God.
That's the nature of fire. It spreads.

You Can't Micromanage a Move of God

Be warned: revival will mess up your schedule.

It will inconvenience your comfort.
It will ruin your reputation with lukewarm Christians.
It may even stir resistance—religious spirits always oppose revival.

But it will be worth it.

Don't put God's fire into a formula. Let it burn on His terms. Trust the process. Stay obedient. Pray longer. Love deeper. Worship louder. Preach Jesus.

Will You Be a Fire Starter or a Fire Extinguisher?

Every believer has the choice.
You can carry oil, or you can carry water.

You can fan the flame, or you can snuff it out with your cynicism.

The question isn't just can revival happen. It's will you be part of it?

The Fire Falls on the Hungry

No one casually drifts into revival.

It comes to those who are desperate. Those who can't go another day without God's presence. Those who hunger more for Jesus than for being liked.

Are you hungry?
Are you ready?

Because the God of fire is still looking for burning ones.

One Thing to Remember

You don't need to be famous to change the world. You just need to be on fire.

One Step to Take

Pray this today:
"Lord, light a fire in me that never goes out. Use me to bring revival wherever I go. Let me be bold enough to burn, and humble enough to stay close to You. I surrender it all."

Now act on it. Call the prayer meeting. Preach the Gospel. Start the spark.

One Scripture to Read Again

"They saw what seemed to be tongues of fire that separated and came to rest on each of them. All of them were filled with the Holy Spirit and began to speak in other tongues as the Spirit enabled them."
—Acts 2:3-4

NEXT STEPS IF YOU ARE READY

What You Do Next Could Shape Eternity

If you've made it to this page, something has already shifted inside you.

Maybe you've repented of your sins. Maybe you've surrendered your life to Jesus.
Maybe you're still trembling—raw, wide-eyed, and overwhelmed by the weight of what's just happened.
Good. That's what a holy moment feels like.

You just made the most important decision of your life.

But hear this clearly: this decision was never meant to be the finish line. It's the starting gun.
You're not just saved from something. You're saved for something.

God didn't rescue you so you could return to business as usual. He called you out of darkness so you could walk in His marvelous light.
He lit a fire in your soul that was never meant to flicker out.

Now it's time to fan that flame.

The next steps you take will either feed that fire or smother it. They will either launch you deeper into the life God created you for or lull you back into the lukewarm comforts He just rescued you from.

Don't go back to sleep. Don't silence the Holy Spirit's voice. Don't wait until you "feel ready."

If Jesus is now your Lord and Savior, these are your marching orders: simple, clear, powerful.

1. Talk to God Like He's Right There Because He Is

Prayer isn't a religious performance. It's not a monologue. It's a lifeline.
You don't need fancy words. You don't need to "sound spiritual." Just be real. Be honest. Be present.

Tell Him your fears.
Tell Him your gratitude.
Tell Him what you don't understand.
And then listen.

God hears every whispered cry. Every groan. Every silent tear. He wants to speak, lead, and walk with you.
You were created for communion. So start today.

2. Start Reading His Word Like Your Life Depends On It

Because it does.

The Bible isn't just a book. It's your sword. It's your map. It's your weapon against the lies of the enemy.
If you want to know God's heart, hear His voice, and walk in His will, you must become someone who feasts on Scripture.

Start in the Gospel of John. Read it slowly. Don't rush. Let the words sink in. Ask the Holy Spirit to open your eyes.
Highlight verses. Write down questions. Wrestle with the hard parts. But stay in it.

Because the moment you step away from God's Word, you start forgetting who you are and why you're here.

3. Find a Bible-Teaching, Jesus-Exalting Church

You weren't meant to do this alone.

You need a local church, not just a podcast or YouTube preacher. You need flesh-and-blood believers who will walk with you, correct you, pray with you, challenge you, and love you in your mess.

Look for a church that:

- Teaches the Bible with authority.
- Exalts Jesus as Lord.
- Welcomes broken people.
- Makes space for the Holy Spirit to move.
- Trains and sends not just entertains.

Don't just attend. Plant yourself. Join a small group. Serve. Be discipled and disciple others. This is your family now.

4. Get Baptized Without Apology

Baptism isn't optional. It's obedience.

It's your public declaration that the old you is dead and the new you has risen with Christ.
It's not about perfection. It's about allegiance. It's your way of saying, "I belong to Jesus and there is no turning back."

Don't wait for the perfect moment. Obey now. Let the world know whose side you're on.

5. Share Your Story Without Fear

You don't need to have a theology degree to be used by God.

You've got something better: a testimony.

Your story of how Jesus saved you, changed you, and lit a fire in your soul could be the very thing that awakens someone else.

Tell it boldly.
Post it.
Text it.
Shout it.
Whisper it at a coffee shop.

Don't let fear silence your redemption story. Somebody's eternity might be waiting on your obedience.

6. Say Yes to the Mission Whatever It Costs

When Jesus saves you, He enlists you.

You are now part of a rescue mission as an ambassador of Heaven with a message the world desperately needs.
You don't need a stage to preach. Your life is the pulpit. Your workplace is the mission field. Your obedience is the sermon.

God will ask you to do hard things. To walk away from sin. To forgive people who hurt you. To open your mouth when it would be easier to stay quiet.

Say yes. Every time.

Say yes when it's uncomfortable.
Say yes when it stretches you.
Say yes when it scares you.

Obedience is where fire falls.

7. Start Living Like Jesus Is Coming Back Because He Is

This world is fading.

Every headline points to what Scripture has warned us about: the end is coming. But you were born for such a time as this.

Live with urgency.
Pray like it matters.
Love like you've been forgiven.
Serve like eternity is at stake.
And don't waste another minute chasing things that won't last.

Jesus is coming and He's coming for a bride who is ready.

FINAL COMMISSION

If this book stirred you…
If the Holy Spirit gripped you…
If you know deep in your bones that this is your moment…

Then don't delay.

Heaven is not impressed by casual faith.
Hell is not afraid of comfortable Christians.

But when one soul says, "Here I am, Lord. Send me" …
Nations can be shaken.
Families can be restored.
Legacies can be rewritten.
Revival can break out.

Let that soul be you.

This is your wake-up call.
Now it's your responsibility.

Get ready. Stay ready.
And help others get ready, too.

Because the trumpet will sound.
And when it does…

You'll be found with your lamp burning.
Your knees worn from prayer.
Your heart steady in the storm.
And your eyes fixed on Jesus.

Let's go!